FLORIDA TERRITORY
IN 1844

FLORIDA TERRITORY IN 1844

THE DIARY

of

Master Edward C. Anderson

United States Navy

Edited with a Foreword and Afterword

by

W. Stanley Hoole

PUBLISHED IN HONOR OF THE
AMERICAN REVOLUTION BICENTENNIAL, 1776—1976,
UNDER THE AUSPICES OF THE
ALABAMA BICENTENNIAL COMMISSION

THE UNIVERSITY OF ALABAMA PRESS
Tuscaloosa

Library of Congress Cataloging in Publication Data

Anderson, Edward C
Florida territory in 1844.

Bibliography: p.
Includes index.
1. Florida—Description and travel—To 1865.
2. Anderson, Edward C. I. Hoole, William Stanley, 1903– II. Title.
F315.A52 917.59'04'4 76-16071
ISBN 0-8173-5036-5 (alk. paper)

Tuscaloosa and London

Contents

Illustrations

In Memory of

WILLIAM BRUNSON HOOLE
(1860–1919)

MARY EVA POWERS HOOLE
(1872–1948)

FLORIDA TERRITORY IN 1844

Edward Clifford Anderson
1815–1883

Foreword

EDWARD CLIFFORD ANDERSON, SON OF GEORGE AND Elizabeth Clifford (Wayne) Anderson, and grandson of the first George Anderson, a sea captain who had forfeited his life during the American Revolution, was born in Savannah on November 8, 1815. From a very early age, even as a growing, barefoot boy in the small but bustling Georgia seaport, he spent many hours playing on and about the river docks, watching the schooners come and go and talking sea-talk with salty old sailors.[1] As far back as he could remember, he wrote in later years, "I longed at an early age to enlist in the United States Navy and become an officer and perhaps a distinguished one in time."[2]

But George Anderson, himself the son of a sea captain who had gone down during the American Revolution, had a different idea concerning his youngest son's destiny. As a widower (his wife, a sister of Associate Justice James M. Wayne of the United States Supreme Court, having died when Edward was "too young to remember her") he had already reared seven other children (three of whom had died) and by now had decided that it would be best for everyone, particularly Edward, for someone else to share the responsibility.[3]

Thus, in the mid-1820's, when an announcement of the newly-established Round Hill School at Northampton, Massachusetts, fell into his hands, he thought he had found the right answer.

Round Hill had been opened on October 1, 1823 by

George Bancroft (soon to become the distinguished historian and later Secretary of the Navy) and Joseph G. Cogswell (the eminent scientist), both former professors at nearby Harvard College.[4] As advertised, Round Hill was no ordinary school. It was open to only a few carefully selected boys, mostly sons of wealthy, prestigious families. The student age limits were from nine to twelve—for it was "with boys rather than young men that Round Hill" was designed. Tuition was $300 annually, including for each scholar "a bed and bed clothes." The method of teaching in this "School for Liberal Education" was modeled after those of Europe, especially Germany and Switzerland, which Bancroft had recently visited. Discipline was strict, studies difficult, punishment severe, schedules precise, and play limited and supervised. According to the Northampton *Gazette*, July 2, 1823,

> [Messrs. Bancroft and Cogswell] intend to have their scholars in the same roof with themselves, whereby they may be able to control all their occupations, and form their habits and morals, as well as cultivate their minds, and thus sustain the relations of both *parents* and *instructors*. No day scholars will be accepted except a limited number from Northampton. They will receive pupils at as early an age as parents are willing to part from them—but they will decline taking charge of any who have passed the age of twelve. They propose to continue the instruction of their pupils so long as it may be deemed expedient, and either fit them to enter on a collegiate course of education, or prepare them to commence their professional studies. The proposed course of instruction embraces the English, Latin, Greek, French, German, Italian, and Spanish languages, mathematics, natural

> history and philosophy, geography, history, ethics, etc. To read and speak English with correctness, will be the first objects of attention.

In short, Round Hill School was all that George Anderson desired for his young son and in 1824 or 1825, when he was ten or eleven, Edward Clifford Anderson was put aboard a sailing vessel in Savannah Harbor, bound via Boston for Northampton on the Connecticut River.[5]

During the eight or nine years that George Bancroft was associated with Round Hill nearly three hundred students were accepted, including day students. Each was hand-picked and carefully screened. Of these students, 177 were from Massachusetts, New York, and Maryland; 34 from South Carolina; 18 from Georgia; 61 from Virginia, North Carolina, Mississippi, Louisiana, Tennessee, Ohio, Michigan, Quebec, Mexico, Brazil, and the West Indies. Among them were James Lathrop Motley (a year older than Anderson—and destined, like Bancroft, to become one of America's noted historians and diplomats) and John Murray Forbes (two years Anderson's senior—and later one of America's railroad magnates), and several sons of the distinguished Carters of Virginia, the Middletons of South Carolina, and the Habershams of Anderson's own State of Georgia.[6]

Needless to say, Round Hillers were closely governed, even to their dress. The daily schedule began at six and ended at eight, every hour filled with study, classes, exercises, and reading the Bible "aloud for relaxation." Students were allowed no pocket money. Teachers were severe and floggings frequent. There was little or no social life. And surely the maturing boys must have longed for permission to visit the young ladies at Mrs. D. Ghuerardi's School for Girls, just a short walk away, in Northampton village.[7]

According to Bancroft's biographer, "the shortcomings and disappointments of Round Hill were many—partly, no doubt, because the institution was too far in advance of its time, and partly by reason of Professor Bancroft's own limitations as a teacher." He was feared, despised, and ridiculed by his pupils. They called him "The Critter" and lampooned him in the school paper by printing a caricature of him "in semblance of a black devil, horned and tailed." Aware of his inadequacies, Bancroft sold his interest in Round Hill to Cogswell in 1830 and, keeping his home in Northampton, devoted his time to politics and to writing his ten-volume *History of the United States*, the first of which appeared in 1834.[8] Alone, Cogswell struggled on with Round Hill, but by 1834 the school had withered away.[9] All together, its life-span was about ten years—but few private schools of its day in so short a time attained such lasting distinction.[10]

The exact dates of Edward Clifford Anderson's tenure at Round Hill cannot be ascertained from extant documents, but it is known that he was there from, say, 1824 to 1830. However, every indication points to the fact that he was painfully unhappy in Northampton and that he returned to Savannah with his determination stronger than ever to become an officer in the United States Navy.

At home Anderson continued his schooling at Chatham County Academy (a semi-private Savannah institution which had been chartered in 1788), living out his boyhood ("which was by no means a remarkably happy one," he confided to his diary), constantly pressured by his stern, unrelenting father to "go through a collegiate course at

Cambridge" and return to the leisurely life of a Georgia plantation owner. But like his grandfather the sea was too much with him and he could not forget it.[11] As he put it, "This feeling grew so strong on me that I neglected my duties & thwarted my Father's wish." And just as he turned eighteen, in 1833, he joyfully wrote, "*I carried my point at last!*"

With the support of Secretary of the Navy Levi Woodbury,[12] Anderson was appointed acting midshipman in the United States Navy on October 20, 1833,[13] and ordered to report on November 1 to the U.S.S. *St. Louis*, a sloop-of-war then riding at anchor in Savannah Harbor.[14]

Following a year's apprenticeship on *St. Louis*, spent mostly in the Gulf of Mexico and the Carribbean Sea, Anderson was commissioned midshipman on November 24, 1834,[15] and assigned to the U.S.S. *Constitution*, Mediterranean Squadron, commanded by Commodore Jesse D. Elliott.[16] During this long tour of duty Midshipman Anderson accompanied Elliott and General Lewis Cass, then United States minister to France,[17] on a three-hundred-mile journey, mostly on horse and mule back, from Jaffa through the Holy Land and back to *Constitution* which had meantime dropped anchor at Tripoli, Lebanon.[18]

Upon the return of "Old Ironsides" to the United States in 1838, Anderson served at the New York, Norfolk, and Philadelphia Navy yards, chiefly on receiving, and hospital ships, on the frigate *Macedonian*, Captain William B. Shubrick,[19] and on the sloops-of-war *Warren*, *Vandalia*, and *Falmouth* in the Home Squadron and the West India Squadron. During these years he cruised from Newfoundland to South America, Europe, and again about the Caribbean Sea and the Gulf of Mexico.[20] On May 16,

1840 he was promoted to passed midshipman.[21]

While on board *Falmouth*, which he joined at the Brooklyn Navy Yard on December 8, 1841, Anderson, now acting master, began keeping an almost daily diary, the first entry of which he dated New York, February 8, 1842. In it he meticulously recorded, not only his personal activities and meditations, but also accounts of events aboard ship, in harbor and at sea, descriptions of vessels, places visited, and many other miscellany. Now and again he entered a poem, original or copied, or made a hand-drawing of a ship, island, fort, flags, landscapes, or, as on one occasion, a drawing of a beautiful but unidentified lady.

Anderson's diary is replete throughout with references to his wife, the former Sarah McQueen Williamson of Savannah (whom he married on February 10, 1841) and their daughter Mary, called Nina (born April 6, 1842), and son Edward Maffitt (born August 6, 1843).[22] His homesickness evidences itself constantly, as does the monotony of his life at sea. Quite often he vented his unhappiness over his failure to win faster promotion in the Navy.[23] From time to time he would occupy his time by sadly reminiscing over voyages past, but, then, in a brighter mood, he would proudly record his ship's fine sailing qualities, one by one describe his shipmates, or express his love of the Navy and his loyalty to the United States.

Anderson's next assignment, following a furlough in the summer of 1842 (which he spent with his family at their Lebanon plantation home near Savannah),[24] was on the U.S.S. *Experiment*, a receiving ship stationed in Philadelphia.[25] There he had leisure time to see the city, attend the theatres, and entertain himself with local politics, in which he took a lively interest. But his loneliness offset his pleasure. He grew increasingly homesick, longing for Sarah, "my darling wife, poor child." On September 9 he wrote, "after all I shall have to quit the service and take care of her, for she is utterly helpless without me."

Sarah was equally lonely and unhappy in Savannah—and she constantly reminded her husband of the fact. In any case, on September 17 she, Nina, and a nurse sailed from Savannah on the brig *Clinton* for New York. Anderson went by train to meet them and escort them to their quarters in Philadelphia. The family remained together there (and later in Brooklyn) until Sarah, Nina, and the nurse returned to Savannah on April 24, 1843.

Meantime, Anderson had in late December been replaced on *Experiment* by Midshipman Daniel Ammen,[26] and assigned to the U.S.S. *Porpoise,* a 224-ton brig in Brooklyn Navy Yard. When he reported for duty, he developed an immediate dislike for the commanding officer, Joshua R. Sands, and soon applied for transfer to the U.S.S. *Truxton,* writing directly to his old friend General Lewis Cass for assistance. He also wrote two letters to Secretary of the Navy Abel P. Upshur, asking his aid, adding that he preferred *Truxton* for several reasons, not the least being that Lieutenant George P. Upshur, the Secretary's brother, was her commander.[27] To his diary, January 9, 1843, Anderson confided that Sands was so incompetent that his own "professional duties whilst actually afloat would be liable to flag under him." With Upshur on *Truxton,* he concluded, "I should have been associated with a man of high principles, & have had the prospect of obtaining *back date,* by means of his influence with his brother."[28]

Thanks to Cass and Upshur, Anderson's transfer from

Porpoise promptly came through—but not to *Truxton* (nor to the U.S.S. *Savannah* which he had stated would be his second choice). Instead, he was assigned as acting master to the U.S.S. *Lexington* which was scheduled to leave in May for a six-months' cruise of the Western Atlantic and the Mediterranean Sea. This appointment, while more desirous than to *Porpoise*, was not prestigious. The 691-ton *Lexington*, eighteen years old, had seen her best days. Built as a sloop-of-war in 1825, she had been stationed in the North Atlantic Squadron and later in the Mediterranean. She had the honor of having brought the body of Commodore Oliver Hazard Perry back to the United States from Trinidad. But more recently, in 1840, she had been converted to a store ship for delivering supplies to fighting vessels throughout the Atlantic.[29]

While awaiting *Lexington's* departure, Anderson grew more despondent. With Sarah and Nina back in Savannah, his loneliness was, as he frequently indicated almost unbearable. On April 28 he wrote his father:

> My dear Sarah and little Mary [Nina] left me on Monday last & have ere this I trust arrived safely at home. Their departure has left me sad & heavy-hearted so much so that I have no spirit left to perform my duties as they should be done. I still look forward to a settlement in life with as much anxiety as ever, and shall avail myself of the first opportunity that affords to do this. I have met with so many disappointments in my profession that I am discouraged and disgusted with it, and only remain for the livelihood which it affords me. I cannot hope under the most favorable circumstances to be promoted to a lieutenancy under four years at the present rate of filling vacancies, and I shall then be unfitted for the situation by the feeling that my promotion has come too late in

> my career. It is the bane of my life to be separated from my family. Let me beg my dear father that you will not misunderstand me in what I have expressed to you. In doing this it is not my wish to distress you by an expression of discontent, nor to ask aid of any kind from you at a time like the present. My object is to get your advice and have you point out to me in what I could best employ myself were I to furlough on the return of this ship [Lexington] to the United States. My great difficulty in writing you is the fact that I cannot do privately, as it is impossible for me to express myself as I otherwise would. I shall be pleased my dear father to hear from you in reply to this letter and to receive such advice as your years and experience shall suggest.[30]

Lexington weighed anchor on May 23, reached the Azores on June 7, sailed along the coast of Portugal into Gibraltar Bay, visited Port Mahon, capital of Minorca in the Belearic Islands, Cape St. Vincent, and other ports, and returned to New York on August 26. During these monotonous months Anderson frequently expressed his longing for home and family. Nor did he fail to lament his failure of being promoted; after a decade, he wrote on June 7, he was still rated master. He was in financial difficulty, his wife's health was ailing, and he was embittered by the nagging knowledge that his father had never forgiven him for joining the Navy rather than attending Harvard. As he put it, he had "been cast adrift by my relatives in so far as to be left to battle the world and *Want*, when they were rolling in wealth, and cannot again look to them for a helping hand."

By September 12, recalling that his pay was only $750 a year, he was even more depressed. "Here I am after eleven years in service in the Navy," he wrote, "with romance narrowed down into sad reality & surfeited up to the throat with disappointment and a sense of injustice. Such is the lot of many another young officer in the service. I entered it with the most enthusiastic feeling and at 22 would not have exchanged a post captain's commission for the Crown of England." And then, sadly, "*Twas my folly!*"

But after a leave which enabled him to spend the winter of 1843–1844 in Savannah and at Lebanon with his "two little chicks," he seemed somewhat more resigned to his situation. Then, on March 16 he received orders to report as sailing master aboard the little, 152-ton coastal steamer, U.S.S. *General Taylor*, then in Savannah. This must have been an unkind cut for a man who had served three and one-half years on the 2,200-ton *Constitution* and nearly six months each on *Lexington* and the 1,341-ton *Macedonian*, commanded by the distinguished Captain Thomas ap C. Jones.[31] For *General Taylor*, an old, shallow-draft, 105-foot craft, only 17½ feet in breadth, which had been used as a troop transport and supply ship in the Seminole Wars, was now ingloriously patrolling the coasts of Florida Territory to keep the Indians quiet and prevent theives from stealing liveoak timber.[32]

As *General Taylor* departed Savannah for Jacksonville, Florida in late March, Master Anderson recorded his thoughts, almost daily, in a small leather-bound ledger. He listed the names, titles, duties, and his opinions of each of the twenty-seven men on board. And during the next nine months, as *General Taylor* cruised up and down and around the east and west coasts of Florida, from one extreme to the other, from Jacksonville to Pensacola, he described the places he visited—Jacksonville, Picalata, Palatka, St. Augustine, the St. Johns River to Lake Munroe, the region about the Miami River, the Florida Keys, Fort Brooke at Tampa, Pensacola, Barrancas, the Perdido River, St. Joseph, and others. His side-trips to historical sites, such as Fort Matanzas, the Indian mounds along the Perdido, and the Minorcan Colony near New Smyrna, he carefully detailed. And his accounts of the slaying of Mrs. Alexander Montgomery by the Indians, his comradeship with General William Jennings Worth, commanding officer of the United States Infantry in Florida, and of Jonathan Walker and William F. English, Florida pioneers, are particularly revealing. All together, they lend a fascinating insight into the military-social life on the peninsula in the mid-1840's.

Master Anderson's Florida Territory diary, which covers the period between March 16 and December 31, 1844, is presented *verbatim* in the pages which follow.

THE DIARY

MARCH 16–DECEMBER 31, 1844

Officers and Men of U.S. Steamer Genl Taylor Employed on the Coast of Florida, 1844

Remarks	*Character*	*Name*	*Rank*
Fussy, hard hearted, fond of popularity	Amiable to a fault	Ebenezer Farrand	Lt Commanding
		Edw[d] C. Anderson	Sailing Master
Understands his profession thoroughly	Sterling Merit	Daniel B. Martin	1st Assistant Engineer
Understands his profession tolerably	Good hearted, but trifling	John Serro (detached)	[2][d] Assistant Engineer
Careless in his duties, but respectful	Uncertain	Henry L. Duer	Pursers Steward
Wayward but very attentive to duty	A good officer	Louis Covetter	Coast pilot
A good accountant, obliging & gentlemanly	Competent when steady	Jessie A. Brush	Capt[s] Clerk
A good mechanic, needs practical Eng[g]	Quiet & gentlemanly	James W. King	3[d] Asst. Engineer
A Drunkard at times, at others steady	A good man, but uncertain	David Brown	Boatswain's Mate
A fine seaman, bold & resolute	Intelligent & respectful	Edward Drew	Signal Qr Master
A tolerably good seam[n]. Not a drunka[d]	Quiet & respectfl. Dull	*Oliver Carpenter	Quarter Master
Very well educated. Son of a Clergyman.	Steady but not a seaman	Warren C. Brown	Quarter Master
Ever at his duty & always respectfl.	Sober, Steady, Obedient	John Sullivan	Fireman
Gets drunk on liberty, never at other times	Excellent & Obedient	W[m] Geary	"do

Remarks	*Character*	*Name*	*Rank*
Quick, active. Desperate when drunk.	So So. Cunning	*Henry Burns	O Seaman
Gets drunk whenever he gets liquor	Worthless. Respectful	John Ware	Seaman
Never knew him intoxicated	An excellent man	Francis Cosimani	O Seaman
An excellent man since he was flogged.	Half witted but do do	David Coleman	Landsman
Very respectful, obedient & quick	An excellent Boy	Henry Charles	O Seaman
Surly, and disposed to play soldier	A sea lawyer	Edward Burrows	do
Quiet, respectful, steady	A good man	*Saml Green	"
Never knew him disobey an order	One of the best in the ship	John Brown	"
Industrious, apt to be imposed on	A *very* good man	Charles Gill	"
Very sober, steady & respectfl	A good servant	Mitchel Vine	"
An old man of wars-man [?]. Unexcept[al]	An excellent man	Joseph McNeale	"
Has behaved remarkably well	Good	Louis Robion (black)	Ships cook
Scrupulously Honest	Honest, but slow	Jas. Williams (black)	Cabin Steward

**Deserted from the Vessel at Blackwater, the former whilst on watch, Dec. 1844.*

1844. Savannah. 16th March, Saturday. Received orders to report to Lt Com[dr] E[benezer] Farrand as actg master of the U S Steamer Genl Taylor,[1] accordingly on friday morning 22[d] repaird on board in obedience to the same & reported. The steamer having got in the evening previous.

On Thursday Morning 28th rose at ½ past 6 am and hurried down to the Exchange wharf opposite which in the stream lay the steamer, hove short & firing up. Got on board immediately. Shortly after 8 we were underway having as passengers Mr Chas Dubignon & Lady & the Hon Thos Butler King.[2] The navigation between Savannah & the St Johns river inland runs through a series of narrow creeks, intersecting the marsh in every direction. It is very uninteresting, being a continuation of flat marsh for miles around, broken occasionally by a knoll of trees, or a stray plantation now and then. We saw, and fired at, many alligators, some of which were struck. Towards sunset passed Frederika [Gen. James E.] Oglethorpes old settlement, some few vestiges of the old foundations are still visible.[3] At half past Seven pm landed Mr King & an hour later sent a cutter up with Mr. Dubignon & his lady, the tide being too low to admit of the Steamers passing through the cut which leads past. Remained at anchor till 3 am, when we got underway & ran down for St Marys Bar.

Friday 29th. We had intended running down the coast for the St John's river, but the weather looking squally and the wind beginning to rise, we bore up & anchored about breakfast time under Amelia island, just abreast of the little town of Fernandina. This is a Spanish settlement, containing some 50 or 60 inhabitants, the town is located on a bluff overlooking the water & is in a state of dilapidation and decay. There were some pretty groves of young orange trees, but not much else worthy of mention. In strolling toward the back part of town I fell in with their burials found and observed that the graves instead of being grown over with grass as with us, were kept bare & planted with flowers. Tis a custom similar to that of the Turks except that with the latter the plants are not set out, but placed in jars fitted into the head of the slab & renewed from time to time as they fade. The weather becoming more strong we abandoned the idea of taking the outside passage & about 12 ock commenced the inland navigation. More tedious as well as lengthy. It rained very hard until sunset, accompanied by thunder & lightning. Our drinking water having been taken from alongside in the Savannah river it was thick & muddy so that I was glad to catch a pitcher full of rain to drink in its place. At six ock in endeavouring to pass through Cincinnati cut we stuck fast in the mud & there remained until the next tide, 4ock am, when we succeeded in getting through.

Saturday. 30th March. At 8 am anchored off Jacksonville (St John's river) where we remained during this day, the wind blowing a gale from South West. This place contains about 600 inhabitants & is one bed of heavy sand.[4]

31st. The high wind of yesterday still continues & the weather cold as mid-winter. At 12 M got underway and ran up to Picolata [25] miles,[5] where we anchored at ½ past 3 pm. On our way up we had quite a fresh breeze from the N.W. There are at present standing in Picolata one large hotel, in a dilapidated condition & another smaller dwelling occupied by an old man named [John Lee] Williams, with his family.[6] These two houses, with an old government stable form the town of Picolata. During the [Seminole] Indian war there were several companies of soldiers stationed here & the large hotel was used as a sort of Barracks for both officers & men. I was shewn the spot where a man had been killed & scalped by the Indians.

1st April the fresh N E gale still continues & a pea jacket indispensable for comfort. The weather looking threatening we ran for a lee under the point whence the bridge is built out, obtained from the shore a pot of fresh milk, about 8 ock pm, the steam boat St Matthews came in from Savannah.[7] Arrived on board this evening Capt H[ezekiah] L. Wistle [Thistle] & suites, dog included. He stalked into the cabin armed to the teeth, having a rifle, brace of pistols, bowie knife & hatchet.[8]

April 2[d] Clear weather. Left Picolata at half past 7 am and in the course of an hour met the St Matthews on her way down the river. Sent a boat alongside of her with letters. 9.40 passed Palataka and at 1.40 anchored off Drayton's island near the entrance of Lake George.[9] We amused ourselves by shooting alligators as we ran along the banks. The country is heavily timbered with oak, ash, cypress &c. After dinner we landed on the island & had a deer hunt. Capt Wistle succeeded in killing a Doe. Found here quantities of oranges, upon which we feasted at pleasure, as they lay strewed upon the ground, rotting in the sun. The trees were also filled with them. They were of a species I had never tasted before viz "bitter sweet" but very palatable & full of juices. A block house built during the Indian war was the only habitation near by, save a Negro house on the premises. An overseer, his wife & one other white man, with three or four negroes live here. They are cultivating the oranges. The soils is composed of shell & earth.

3d. Mild pleasant weather, wind light from S[h] E. 6.30 am left Drayton's island & at 11.50 moored alongside the Bank, at a place called Beresfords Lake, dist from our last stopping place 50 miles. Nothing can surpass the beauty of the scenery which greets the eyes in passing through the streams & inlets of this portion of the country. The woods are clothed in the richest & most delicate green, whilst the rank luxuriance with which vegetation burst forth from wherever there is the slightest soil, fills the beholder with admiration. The banks upon either side are fringed with verdures, springing out of the very water, whilst within may be seen groves of wild orange trees burdened with fruit & flowers. The presence of these groves may be discovered long before being seen, for the trees being at this season in blossom the air is freighted with sweets, so much so as at times to be sickening. Cypress trees of enormous growth tower aloft on either bank, & groves of the Palmetto in turn vary this endless variety of forest scenery. We have not seen as yet any very extensive groves of the live oak, although trees of the largest size are to be met with in every direction. The land varies along the course of the stream, sometimes low in prairie, but not extending inward to any extent & again rising in moderate bluffs & hammocks. We hunted at Beresfords landing, but without success, notwithstanding we saw tracks of deer & turkeys in abundance. Having dined I took a boat & pulled into the neighbouring creeks "bobbing for trout" Capt Peck, our pilot who was with me succeeded in taking 8 very fine ones.[10] There is a settlement on the point of bluff, opposite where our steamer lay which has been partly cleared of its timbers, that is to say there is a small hut without an occupant and the timber lies felled on the ground. The location is an extremely pretty one & is probably in the possession of one of the "armed occupants" who to secure a right to the land is obliged to cultivate the soil for a period not less than five years. This can be accomplished by merely felling a few trees & then planting from year to year without reaping, after which he may receive his grant & sell at a profit to whoever may be disposed to purchase. Gave chase to a large flock of wild turkees in the hope of driving them into the trees, but could not get a shot at them. Later in the evening accompanied Capt Farrand in search of the same flock. Landed near the spot where I had started them & ranged the woods with Capt Thistle. Got into the heart of the swamp & saw a deer, but could not get a shot at him. Later than this I got into the cutter and pulled high up the stream. Ere we returned, the sun had set & the dark shadows of the trees, thrown upon the water gave to the scene an air of solemnity that was both pleasing & impressing. Rounding a point of the river we passed a grove of orange trees, the odour from which was delightful. Pity that a country abounding in so much that is beautiful should nourish from its very luxuriance all that is pestilential & sickly. I am inclined to believe that it can never be thickly peopled & certainly not so until the vast quantity of vegetable matter shall be cleared away. Even then the rays of a hot sun acting upon the moist land left bare by the removal of the forests will produce miasma worse than poison. Old Thistle & his man Grimes started off on a fine hunt, but got nothing.[11]

4th April. Clear mild weather, musquitos very troublesome during the night. 4.30 am left Beresford Lake & ran 8 miles up the river to a place called the Blue Spring. This is a sulphur spring rising some two or three miles from where we came to. The water is very clear, emitting a strong smell & becoming more transparent as you approach the head of the spring. The bottom of the channel leading to the spring is strewn with trees which have fallen in from time to time. They are coated with sulphur, as was the back of a terrapin which I saw paddling about in the creek. Found on the bluff where we moored two men felling timber for a clearing. Left there at 9.30, & came to in the upper Weekiva where we filled our water casks from the stream. Shot some very large alligators on the passage up, also a number of birds &c. There are three small rivers bearing the name of Weekiva. This is the upper one. It empties into the St Johns & its water as you approach the head is clear and limpid. Taking the cutter we followed its windings until it lost itself in a narrow brook, clear as crystal. There were other sources however, but this seemed to be the main. The banks are pretty, being fringed with green & in some spots festooned with vines drooping from the trees, on either side huge cypresses overhang the water, few of which measure less than 12 feet in circumference & many of them 30 at the base. One of these trees felled by Capt Farrand for a canoe is of this size.

On the 6th April, at sunset we left the Weekiva and passing through into Lake Munroe, came to anchor, opposite fort Mellon,[12] abreast of a settlement owned by a person named "Major Taylor,"[13] at 8 pm. Took the cutter and two men & pulled inshore fishing with the cast net, caught nothing and returned on board about 11. We remained at the place over Sunday, our object in coming this far being to enable Thistle to ascertain the amount of depradation committed by the live oak cutters. About ten I landed. The soil seems to be poor & is thickly strewn with the Palmetto. The fences in the quarter being made of it. There are some ten or a dozen people living here & a large commodious boarding house for invalids, the numerous sulphur springs in the immediate premises inducing the owner to put up so large a dwelling in the hope of getting strangers down here. One of these springs is remarkable. It lies some hundred yards from the beach, in the woods & is a basin oblong in form & measuring 55 yards by 65. It has been sounded with a line 112 feet in length without finding bottom. The water is white sulphur, with a strong mixture of lime I should judge. People in the neighbourhood assert that the Indians considered these springs as being on holy ground & consequently allowed none but the sick to reside in their neighborhood. They are certainly very tempting to the eye for bathing & not very palatiable to swallow. Got on board by noon & after dinner sent to the beach & obtained a barrel full of snail shells for Nany.[14] At this settlement we procured some fresh milk, we are now 225 miles from the mouth of the river.

7th Bade adieu to Major Taylor & his reputed villany. At 7.15 am and moved down to the mouth of the Lake. A party of us took to the woods after breakfast in search of an orange grove, but returned after a most wearisome tramp without finding one. I got a shot however at a deer and wild turkey, but they were both too far off to hit. The memorable tramp (for it tired me almost to death) took us into the piny woods, through palmetto hammocks and worse than all through palmetto *scrub.* Upon the representation of one of the "armed occupants" that he would conduct us into a grove where the "bitter sweets" abounded, accordingly I took three men with me with bags to be filled & made the poor devils lug them along to the last. When finding that my citizen friend "the armed occupant" was evidently on a wild goose chase I retraced my steps & got on board nearly dead with thirst & quite melted up. We saw at the landing notches that had been cut in the trees by the Indians during the war for the purpose of resting their rifles in, and I was told that a band of them had lain in wait there for sometime expecting that the troops would make a descent on that point, but fortunately or unfortunately as the case may be, no such event occurred. Lake Munroe is six miles long & from 3 to 3½ in width, depth about one fathom average. Coasts level & timbered with pine, palmetto cypress and oak. Proceeding down we came again to our old stopping place opposite the mouth of the Weekiva & after taking on board a canoe for the Captain which had been hewn on its banks, continued on our course down the river as far as Drayton's island. At this place we stopped to procure oranges, vast groves of which are growing wild on the opposite main. A party left the vessel to hunt deer, whilst I took a boat & went to the orange grove. It is situated some 50 yards from the beach and is so dense that it requires good navigation to get through the underwood. The air is almost excluded in consequence & the heat is oppressive. The orange trees are all small in size but very luxuriant & so covered with fruit & blossoms as to burden the atmosphere & render it disagreeably sweet. We found both the bitter sweet & sour & after filling the boat left the earth strewn with oranges. The hunters returned on board unsuccessful, but the next morning old Thistle succeeded in bringing down a noble buck upon which we feasted many days after.

On the 10th April continued on our way down the river & at 1.15 ran alongside the wharf at Palatka where we remained a quarter of an hour. There are large storehouses here, built by [the] Government during the Florida war when it was drawing to a close. They belong at present to the heirs of a Dr. [Charles W.] Brush,[15] having been erected on his land with the understanding that as soon as the war was over all improvements etc were to left standing. They are going to decay, for nobody takes any care of them. Hence we ran into Black Creek, a fine body of water & landed at sunset at a place some ten or 12 miles up belonging to one of the "armed occupants," an industrious, decent fellow for he gave us a turkey. We filled our water casks in the creek and found it the best we have as yet obtained. From Black Creek, passed into the St Johns again & arrived at half past nine in the evening at Jacksonville where we anchored & remained until the following sunset. Dined with Dr. [Henry D.] Holland, formerly of Savannah & received from Mr. Dayton my account which had been sent to Dr H's care by Mr [Henry R.] Sadler.[16]

12th at 6.30 pm ran down to St Johns bar and anchored, got underway at 5.15 the next morning, passed out to sea in a dense fog and at half past eleven arrived in St Augustine harbour. Old associations thick and strong came over me for when I last was here I was upon the point of being married & felt lovesick even into death. The place has not improved much since my visit except in the erection of the new barracks & completion of the sea wall. This last extends all along the front of the town & protects it from the encroachment of the sea which otherwise in heavy gales from the eastward would break into the city. Four companies of the 8th Infantry under the immediate command of Genl [William Jennings] Worth, are stationed in the Barracks.[17] They are the best looking American troops I have seen, but from all accounts an insubordinate set of scoundrels. They cannot compare to the British troops in point of appearance & no soldiers that I have ever met with yet have. Genl Worth keeps his men in full harness constantly & drills them every morning. We see them from the vessel & they make quite a pretty appearance. Their band is only so, so. The most interesting building in St Augustine is the old Spanish fort [Matanzas] a fine piece of masonry, built

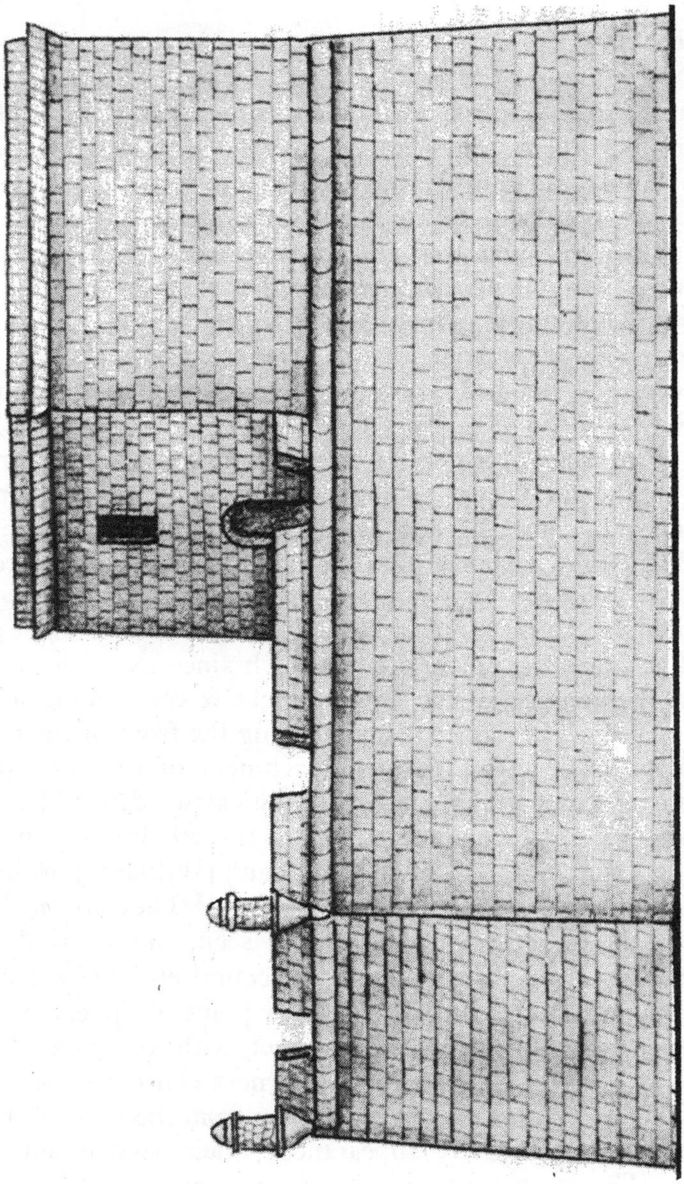

Anderson's Drawing of Fort Matanzas

during the early settlement of the country, years ago when all our flourishing states were colonies. It is of the shell stone of the region and like all Spanish forts built with great art and symmetry. During the Florida War it was garrisioned by the United States troops, but since they they have been withdrawn to the Barracks.[18] Coacochee, the Indian chief was confined there & escaped through a loop hole by letting himself down with his blankets, he is represented to have been the very best specimen of an Indian warrior. After his escape he kept the whole neighbourhood in constant alarm & committed more cruelties than any chief of his nation. Tis said that he did this in revenge for some ill treatment received during his captivity.[19]

On Tuesday the 16th of April at half past six in the morning, hauled alongside the pier & at nine took on board the community of St Augustine en masse, bound on a pleasure excursion.[20] This party was gotten up by the captain in consequence of some promise to a portion of his acquaintances. We had the band from the Garrison and danced & made merry until nine pm. There were many pretty girls on board, very sociable & quite agreeable. I formed some very pleasant acquaintances among them & struck up two friendships in the Misses Bairds. We proceeded to the old Fort at Matanza's & there anchored until 3 ock. This is a square sort of tower intended by the Dons to defend a passage to the sea in old times. There are four embrasures for cannon in the lower parapet, and one old dismounted twelve pounder mouldering on the platform. An additional elevation rises in the West side of this plateau forming a perpendicular to the beach, the whole is grown over with weeds & is going rapidly to decay. The access is by ladders, which in old times were hauled up at sunset. The upper portion was to be reached only in the same manner. Many of the ladies ventured up the first battlement & some few even got as high as the second. Twas in bad taste I thought, for the wind was blowing almost a gale at the time and the exposé was hazardous. We had intended having a kind of picnic here, but the place was too wild for so large a party. The ladies therefore crossed the river for a walk on the sea beach. I remained behind with two army officers to eat oysters &c. We had a roast & then returned on board. As we were getting alongside I was requested for "particular reasons" to take one of a select party about to stroll on the beach. I accepted of course, but never discovered the "particular reasons" except in having been given to understand that a lady requested it. We got back to St Augustine at 9 pm & after putting everybody on shore hauled out into the stream near our old moorings. Altogether twas a pleasant affair, we had some sweet songs on the guitar & some very quiet little flirtations. I was pleased when they all left & yet then came one of those terrible revulsions to which I am almost invariably subjected after gayety, that calm in the feeling which seems to mock at the pleasures of life and tell us that the levity of today cannot avert the sad realities which may be in store for us.

Tuesday 19 April. Proceeded to sea having on board Genl Worth & suite, consisting of Lt [Jacob E.] Blake, A[rthur] T. Lee, U S A passed Mid Marine,[21] an orderly sergeant & a servant. Genl W is on his way to Cuba on some official business. We found him quite an agreeable person & very intelligent in all respects. He is perhaps the best officer in the army, combining great personal energy with a ripe and excellent judgement. I draw this conclusion first from his ability in closing the Florida war and next from his bearing & deportment which is very soldierly, his keen black eye took my fancy from the first and I observed that in addressing persons he has a habit of looking fixedly at them as though he wished them to quail before his glance. I decided at once to meet his eye whenever he spoke to me & to give back the same steady gaze so peculiar to him. At the same time never to proffer conversation to him whether this pleased him or not I can't say, but we struck up a great friendship for each other. My vanity does not lead me to this assertion, because I have been told by several persons that "the General was very much pleased with me." Genl W has his faults too in common with the rest of us. He is decidedly a vain man & I should judge him to be a passionate one.

Our passage outside was pleasant. We kept in sight of the coast all the way and on Sunday 21st at 2 pm anchored off the mouth of the Miami River.[22] Our object in stopping here was to procure wood, but as no supply was to be had we remained only until breakfast time the next morning. The neighbourhood of this place is remarkable for a species of bulbous root called by the Indians, Coonti & valued by them beyond everything. It produces flour of the whitest and most beautiful discription.[23] So highly did the Seminoles regard this plant that in their treaty with the United States government they for a long time besought for the privilege of returning here at stated periods to gather it & if possible retain it in their limits. It was refused. Genl Worth told me that they contended longer for this than for any other stipulation, alas the poor Indian, such has it ever been. So will it always be. After leaving Miami we continued our course South until nine pm, when we anchored in 3 fthms water abreast of Indian Key. On our run we caught from time to time some very fine King fish. They are fine eating. Genl W. and myself concocted a chowder, but the steward spoiled it. Numberless wreckers are hovering around in search of prey. These gentlemen live upon the misfortunes of others & look forward to the season when vessels are driven on the reefs with the same anxiety that a planter may be supposed to anticipate the harvesting of his crop. They form a community peculiar to themselves & live mostly upon Key West and the adjoining islands or as they are termed, Keys. They cruise about in small sloops & have quite a considerable capital invested in their particular business. As soon as it is rumored aboard that a wreck is on the reefs, it produces a general excitement and bustle in the island. Every man and boy puts off and the first alongside makes the bargain whereby he is insured so much for lightening the vessel & saving so much of the cargo. In some respects then they are useful, yet still they fatten on the mishaps of others. Fancy a fellow whilst saying grace over a meal, looking forward in his heart for some richly laden merchantman to founder on the rocks. I was shewn a "wrecker" who never sat down to a meal without asking a blessing.

On the 23d April, at 1.15 pm anchored off Key West & after dinner accompanied Gen W at his request to visit the Barracks.[24] We went up in one of their boats. The buildings are all new & constructed with piazzas running round the houses. They are still incomplete. A salute was fired on our landing. I met here Lt [Charles G.] Merchant & Mr & Mrs Beardsley the latter fellow passengers of Sarah's in his trip from New York to Savannah on board the brig Philura. . . . [25] Key West has nothing attractive about it. It is a sandy waste with some scrub timber upon it & in the town a scattering of plantain &

banana trees, giving it a tropical appearance. There are several comodious warehouses here in which goods from wrecked vessels are stored away. In one of them was a room used as a Theatre. To while time we formed a party & went to see the play. Admission one dollar. The performance was the best *unintential burlesque* upon performances in general that could possibly be enacted. The chief actor had no teeth & the hero of the piece (dressed in a red uniform coat with two epaulets) I saw the next day loafing about the docks. Return[d] on board at half past ten & took Gen W with me. We met at the billiard room. After we got quickly seated in the cabin he proposed to me to accompany him to Cuba & asked me if I thought Capt Farrand would be authorised to detach me on that service, to join his vessel again on her return to Key West. I replied that I thought not, being the only officer on board. Had I felt the inclination to have gone however Gen W[s] request to Capt F with an official letter to him, would have settled the matter directly, but I preferred continuing on my present service because it will ensure my meeting Sarah sooner & beside that it is proper that I should remain, there being no emergency requiring me to go to Cuba. I have quite forgotten to mention Judge [William A.] Marvin, he came with us from St Augustine to this place and is the U S arbiter in cases of salvage.[26] The Judge had been to St Augustine on a matrimonial expedition, intending I am told to return with his bride to Key West, but the lady in the mean while changed her mind.

On the 25th of April at daylight left Key West and continued our course for Tampa. We caught on the way several fine King fish by towing lines astern. They are quite a delicacy. The following morning at 4 ock, ran almost high & dry on a sandbank off Sara Soto, but succeeded without difficulty in heaving her afloat again. Arrived at Fort Brooke,[27] Tampa Bay at 1 pm 26th. Genl Worth and suite here took leave of us. Although pleasant and agreeable men all of them I was not sorry to be once again freed from the restraint which the presence of strangers necessarily imposes. Marines remained on board with us at my invitation until it should be time for us to leave. Lee is an amusing fellow & I should suppose an excellent soldier.[28] He has been engaged in several skirmishes with the Indians & mentioned to me an anecdote of a soldier which is worth relating here. Being on a scout upon one occasion they fell in with & were fired on by a party of Indians in ambush. Immediately as was customary in that species of warfare he ordered each man to take a tree. All obeyed but one man & he proudly drawing himself up exclaimed "I am an English Soldier, Lieutenant, I never did such a thing in my life & I cannot do it now." He escaped uninjured. The fellow was worthy of knighthood. I saw him at St Augustine when we were there as a musician in the regimental Band.

Tampa, or more properly the Military reserves is a charming spot. It is overgrown with huge old oaks spreading their arms abroad in every direction & giving a shade which is at all seasons delightful.[29] There differ from the oaks usually seen with us being trimmed in such a way as to leave the body & arms of the tree bare until they spread over to an enormous extent & then the foliages & the moss droop down from the branches. There are four companies of the 8th infantry stationed here. The officers are poor looking men with but one exception, Capt [Richard B.] Scriven. Soon after leaving the vessel Gen Worth sent down to request our company to dinner at Col [William

G.] Belknaps.[30] We saw on reaching his quarters a small party of Seminole Indians who had come in from their camp to have a "talk" with the Genl. They were a villianous looking set, without one redeeming trait about them. They conversed through a negro interpreter, Sampson & talked about their crops &c &c., only replying however to such questions as were put to them.[31] This Sampson by the way is the very beau ideal of a handsome fellow, his features were perfect & his figure, thin, lithe, graceful, dressed in the Indian costumes. I thought him one of the finest if not the finest looking man I had ever seen. On the second day we dined again with Genl W. & after dinner rode out for a few miles into the country. The neighborhood is grown over with the short tangled palmetto & scrub & afforded during the war a safe ambuscade to the Indians for it was impossible to catch them & from there coverts they shot down without mercy all small parties & single travellers that ventured on the road. I was mounted on a powerful express horse, but his best days were over.

Remained at the Reserve until sunset and then dropped down to the wood landing, five miles distant. Next morning I took my gun & landing abreast of the vessel strolled up along the beach in search of game, shells, or whatever else might be met with. The shore was lined with common coral, but I saw no specimens worth picking up. There was a singular flower growing near the margin of the water of a brilliant purple colour, resembling in form the verbena. I plucked a parcel of them & took them on board. The morning was intensely hot with the glare from the water almost insupportable, but I continued on along the beach for upwards of a mile & then returned to the vessel having seen nothing strange but a sulphur spring & a flock of sandpipers which I fired into. The Indian Chief Billy Bowlegs arrived into Tampa the afternoon we left the Reserve. I did not see him.[32]

Left Tampa at 10.35 am (Monday 29th April) and on the following evening anchored off the town of St Joseph's. The night was clear & beautiful but we were obliged to steer for the anchorage entirely by our bearings on the chart as no light could be discerned in any direction.

Wednesday May 11th 1844. Landed at St Joseph and strolled through the town. Twas really a melancholy saunter, for the place had been deserted by the inhabitants and had an air of gloom out of keeping with our age of prosperity. Fine dwellings, finished in the best style have been abandoned by their owners and left to rot piecemeal in the weather. Windows & doors are gaping open swinging to & fro with every gust. The grass grows rankly in the streets and wolves and bears now prowl when only a few years ago was all the bustle & excitement of business. The place was in its prime remarkable for good society and gayety. It was built to break down Apalachicola & a costly wharf & railroad constructed to facilitate the transfer of goods which its fine harbour led the inhabitants to believe that vessels would flock in to take away. For a short time their expectations were realized.[33] Property rose to an exhorbitant value & houses were put up on a corresponding scale, but in the meantime they had exhausted their funds. The railroad was mismanaged & when the revulsion came the inhabitants found themselves invalid in ruin & left the place in disgust. Others followed until all went away but a few families & when we arrived there in the steamer we found those few preparing to go away. Houses that cost twelve & fourteen thousand could be bought for one hundred & so dreary was the prospect that a gentleman wishing to sell out a comfortable dwelling was offered by a tailor a frock coat for it. The window sashed, doors &c of many of the houses have been taken away thus rendering the desolation the more conspicuous. Three men with a cart & horse were so engaged as we passed along. One of them, a wild looking savage came up & asked if we would purchase some bear meat from him, as he had killed one that morning fresh & fat. Met at this place a Dr Price & his wife,[34] acquaintances of Mrs Jones', they were on the eve of departure for Texas. At noon left St Joseph's passed out to sea & stood away to the Westward for Pensacola.[35]

Thursday May 2^d^ at 3 am came to anchor off the Navy Yard, found the [U.S.S.] Poinsett anchored there. No other man of war. The French corvette Brilliante at the Town. Capt [Elia A. F.] Lavallette commands the station & is very unpopular. I found him however extremely courteous & gentlemanly in my intercourse with him.[36] There are evidently two factions in the yard, of which the unpopular one is in the ascendant. The enclosure has been very much beatufied of late years & has a range of buildings for the accommodation of the officers & their families.

On friday the 3^d^ the Poinsett went to sea, with a bearer of dispatches for Mexico.

Saturday 4th Got underway at 6.30 am & stood out to sea, found myself for the first time in command of a United States vessel at sea, Capt F having gone over to his family. Ran to the Westward as far as Perdido Bar, sounded it and passed over into the river carrying not less than 7 feet. Stood up to the Weehawk Bayou & moored head & stern there, abreast of Capt F's house. I can say but little in favour of the Perdido.[37] Tis a naval settlement

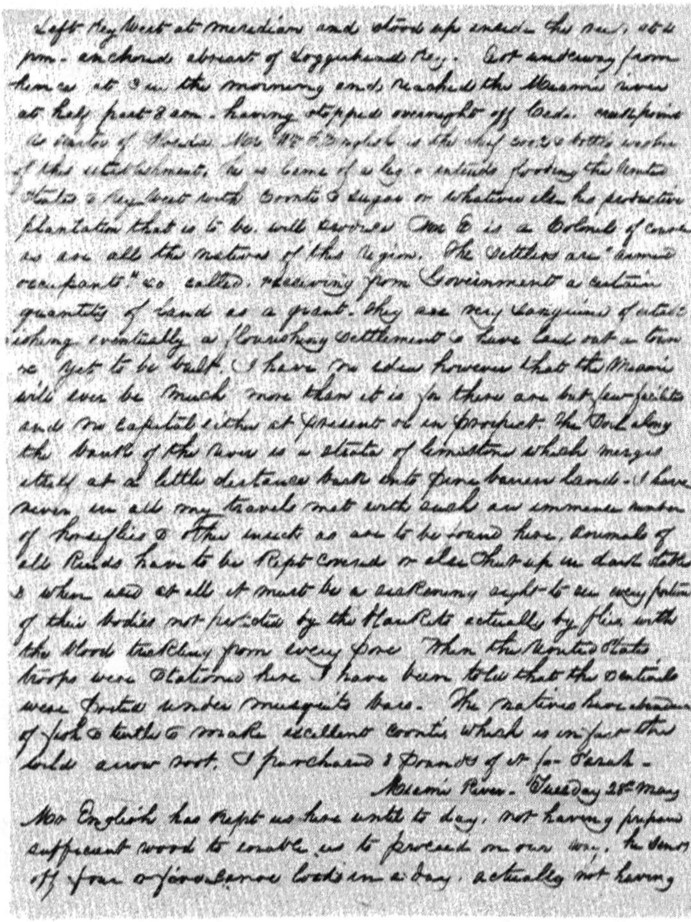

Left Key West at meridian and stood up under the reef, at 4 pm. anchored abreast of Loggerhead Key. Got underway from hence at 3 in the morning and reached the Miami river at half past 8 am. having stopped overnight off Cedar [illegible] the [illegible] of Florida. Mr. Wm. F. English is the chief [illegible] & [illegible] of this establishment, he is [illegible] of a big & extensive [illegible] flooding the United States & Key West with Coontie & sugar or whatever else the prospective plantation that is to be will produce. Mr. E. is a Colonel of course as are all the natives of this region. The settlers are "armed occupants" so called, receiving from Government a certain quantity of land as a grant. They are very sanguine of establishing eventually a flourishing settlement & have laid out a town [illegible] yet to be built. I have no idea however that the Miami will ever be much more than it is for there are but few facilities and no capital either at present or in prospect. The soil along the banks of the river is a strata of limestone which merges itself at a little distance back into pine barren lands. I have never in all my travels met with such an immense number of horseflies & other insects as are to be found here, animals of all kinds have to be kept covered or else shut up in dark stables & when used at all it must be a sickening sight to see every portion of their bodies not protected by the blankets actually by flies with the blood trickling from every pore. When the United States troops were stationed here I have been told that the sentinels were posted under musquito bars. The natives have abundance of fish & turtle & make excellent Coontie which is in fact the wild arrow root. I purchased 8 pounds of it for Sarah.

Miami River. Tuesday 28th May

Mr English has kept us here until to day, not having prepared sufficient wood to enable us to proceed on our way, he [illegible] off four or five canoe loads in a day, actually not having

PAGE FROM ANDERSON'S DIARY, MAY 25, 1844

in the piny woods and promises fair from the number of small children I saw around there, to be populous one of these days. We remained nine days during which time our men were employed on shore in cutting wood. Rather severe work for this season of the year & not just, since it is a service for which poor Jack did not enlist, and if persisted in will put more than one poor devil under the sod. On the Sabbath preceding our departure Capt F gave a pleasure jaunt to the natives of the Perdido, a motley crew. Blue Devils & Grey—Black Devils & Brown, to say nothing of sundry small children.

Monday 13th May '44. Left the Perdido at 7 am and stood slowly down towards the mouth of the river. In attempting to pass the Bar we grounded on it & remained firmly imbedded nearly an hour and a half, ran out a small kedge & endeavoured to heave her off, but this not succeeding lowered the larboard bower anchor into the boat. A sea rolled in, filled her, upset her & tore her in two, precipitating the men in her overboard. One seaman was carried under with the anchor but not injured. After much difficulty succeeded in backing her off. Ran into the river, moored beside the bank, got in & repaired the boat. At sunset I shoved off in her to sound the bar, but accomplished nothing. Picked up an oar that I had thrown over in the morning to the men in the water also the boats rudder, &c, &c. Next morning at daylight, again sounded the channel, placed a buoy at the deepest point which was only four & a half feet. Got underway & attempted to pass out. Again grounded & only got over the bar by throwing overboard wood & running out kedges. I trust this may be our final experiment at the Perdido Bar. Arrived at Pensacola Yard at 9.30 am. Found anchored there the U S Brig Somers. Her commander Capt [James T.]

Gerry came on board & offered me the second Lieutenancy of her as he was in need of officers which I declined.[38] At the Yard we took in stores, provisions etc.

Thursday 16th May '44. The Brig Somers went to sea this morning, bound to Galveston. By her first Lieut I sent Purser Bryans letter & parcel, entrusted to me by his wife. At 8 pm we followed her & commenced our retrograde run down the coast.

Saturday 18th at 4 pm Stood in to Tampa Bay & at 8 anchored some miles below the military post.

19th Shifted our berth at 5.30 am & ran within four miles of the Reserve. Sent a boat up & by her return received dear Sarahs letter of the [blank] forwarded from St Augustine by the polite attention of Lt [John T.] Sprague, Genl Worths son in law.[39] At 10.20 got underway, ran down to the Manatee river, entered this stream & anchored 6 miles from its mouth for the purpose of procuring wood, that engaged at Tampa having been sold to the Cincinnati. Remained here till noon of Tuesday 21st. There appear to be a number of settlers on the banks of this river but whether they will every come to anything remains a problem. The lands are considered good for the culture of sugar. Passed out to sea & steered to the S[d] & E[d].

Thursday 25th. Anchored back of the middle ground at 12.30 am. Key West light bearing S S E. Weighed anchor at 7.40 & came to off Key West wharf at 8.15 am. Left Key West at meridian and stood up inside the reef. At 4 pm anchored abreast of Loggerhead Key. Got underway from hence at 3 in the morning and reached the Miami river at half past 8 am, having stopped overnight off Cedar Creek point. A senator of Florida, Mr Wm F. English is the chief cook & bottle washer of the establishment, he is lame of a leg & intends flooding the United States & Key West with Coonti & sugar or whatever else his productive plantation that is to be will produce. Mr E is a Colonel of course as are all the natives of this region. The settlers are "armed occupants," so called, receiving from Government a certain quantity of land as a grant. They are very sanguine of establishing eventually a flourishing settlement & have laid out a town &c yet to be built.[40] I have no idea however that the Miami will ever be much more than it is for there are but few facilities and no capital either at present or in prospect. The soil along the bank of the river is a strata of limestone which merges itself at a little distance back into pine barren land.[41] I have never in all my travels met with such an immence number of horseflies & other insects as are to be found here. Animals of all kinds have to be kept covered or else shut up in dark stables & when used at all it must be a sickening sight to see every portion of their bodies not protected by the blankets actually by flies, with the blood trickling from every pore. When the United States troops were stationed here I have been told that the sentinels were posted under musquito bars. The natives have abundance of fish & turtle & make excellent coonti, which is in fact the wild arrow root. I purchased 8 pounds of it for Sarah.

Miami River, Tuesday 28 May. Mr English has kept us here until to day, not having prepared sufficient wood to enable us to proceed on our way, he sends off four or five canoe loads in a day, actually not having energy enough to stop a rent in a flat by which means he might have saved the labour of two working hands & furnished our fuel in half the time. Left the Miami at 5 am & attempted to pass out through Bears Cut, but failed & followed the usual channel out to sea. We had a fine fair wind all this day, with blue water & a heavy sea, an agreeable change to one who has been feeling his way through the soapy looking stuff around the reefs.

Arrived at Musquito at noon on Wednesday 29 & proceeded up to the Fort, so called, 3½ miles from the sea.[42] Two brigs & a schooner were on shore on the Bar, one of them high and dry at low water. We passed in having at the lowest cast five feet, drawing very nearly that. Four vessels laden with live oak were in the mouth of the river waiting to go out & two others at the Fort loading. Musquito Bar shifts with every gale of wind & is considered in rough weather one of the worst, if not the very worst on the whole coast of Florida. Fortunately the inducement for crossing it are not frequent, there being no calls for vessels to touch here except for those specially employed by the live oak cutters, they generally insure, but the difficulties of the bar are such as to deter captains from making an engagement more than once. Three wrecks on a bar are enough to frighten one. The settlement such as it is is known by the name of New Smyrna. The remains of a once splendid house are still to be seen on its right bank going up, it was built at an enormous outlay of money & burnt by the Indians after the breaking out of the war. The river is remarkable for the quantity & quality of fish found in its waters. With a cast net we procured a boat load in a very short time. There are fine oysters to be obtained here & in my case they were got at the cost of one or two severe gashes in the fingers, for having wandered along the shore without a knife I was obliged to use a shell to open them with. Remained at Musquito until Monday morning 3^d^ of June when we left for St Augustine. During our stay at New Smyrna we towed to sea the following vessels laden with live oak for the U S Government, viz on Thursday May 30th at 4.30 pm, Brig Frendaskegg [?]—Friday 31st at 5.30 Brig Canary. Sunday 2^{d} June at 6 am, schooner Brace & Monday 3^{d} at 7.45 schooner Hope.

Monday 3^{d} June 1844. At 9.20 am after casting off the schooner Hope hauled up to the Nd & W^{d} and arrived safely after a pleasant run up the coast at St Augustine off which we anchored at 5 pm. Getting up thus far North seems like approaching home again. Soon after anchoring I landed and called on Genl Worth, he was at table with some guest of his but the moment I entered he rose from his seat and advanced into the passage to meet me. His greeting was cordial in the extreme and after shaking me warmly by the hand he again caught it to renew his welcome. Capt F kindly gave me "leave" to return to Savannah without delay and accordingly I had engaged a seat in the mail for the next morning to start at 6, but about 2 am a person from the shore hailed the boat to say that he had a message for the Captn from Genl W. Being restless & nervous at the prospect of starting for home in the morning the hail awoke me, but the quarter master came in immediately to report to me. I directed him to enquire whether the message from Genl Worth would not keep till a more seasonable hour in the morning. The reply being in the negative a boat was sent to the wharf & Capt Sprague, the Genl's aid and son in law stepped on board. According to him the Genl had but just received an order to repair to the North immediately and as it was impossible for him to get ready in time to reach the boat at Picolata, he begged as a great favour that Capt F would run up to Savannah with him, a modest request truly. Now this though it suited me precisely inasmuch as it took me home some 24 hours sooner than I could otherwise have reached there, did not correspond at all with my notions of propriety for I think it argued an inclination to make a convenience of the vessel and officers, besides evincing a want of delicacy in the request & anxious as I was to arrive at home I felt disappointed when I heard the captain asquiesce. The Genl has a peculiar way of his own in such matters, though I cannot say that I admire him the more for it. I had promised on leaving him to return in the morning and breakfast with him, as he would take no refusal, so after stopping at the stage office to give up my seat I called at his house & finding the family not astir (for it was early) left word that I would not be able to join him. I learned afterward that he had intended sending me over to Picolata in his carriage, had not the change in the destination of the boat rendered it unnecessary. As it was the Captn & myself were to dine with him so at half past two I found myself in his drawing room conversing with his daughter, Mrs Sprague. She had but recently been confined, but her face bore no marks of illness. There is something pleasant about this lady. She is young but possesses a good deal of womanly dignity besides being very beautiful. This is a first impression. I am careful in this noting it, because I never met with a person in my life who upon acquaintance did not materially change. Four or five officers of the army, with a Mr [George W.] Cole, formerly a paymaster in it,[43] were the generals guests on this day. This last gentleman has accumulated a fortune from his vocation. We did not sit over our wine, as this was one of the conditions of our acceptance, so as soon as the cloth was removed I reminded Capt Farrand that our time had expired and left them to go on board & get the steamer alongside the dock.

June 4th. At 4.40 pm ran alongside the dock, took on board Genl Worth, Major [Eugene] Van Ness, Lieut Sprague & Major [LeGrand] Capers.[44] Left St Augustine and stood down for the Bar, passed it at 5.30 and at 6 took the bearing of the light house, SW ¼ S, dist 5 miles. Steered North, at 8.25 made St Johns light on the Larboard bow at 9 pm passed abreast of it. At 11 passed St Mary's Light. At midnight I was roused to relieve the pilot. The moon was shining brightly and with a smooth sea we were speeding away for Tybee [Island]. How my heart seemed to beat with the rapid revolution of the wheels. Could I have looked a little into the future what a sad middle watch it would have been to me.

Wednesday June 5th. A clear sunny morning. At 9 running along Ossabaw island, soon after this made Tybee light, passed into the river at 11 and anchored off the [Savannah] Exchange at 1 pm. On our way up a steamer with flags & music ran by us bound on a pleasure excursion to the rivers mouth. A large number of ladies & gentlemen were on board, but I recognized no acquaintance. The boat tolled her bell to us in passing, according to merchant custom but we took no notice of the courtesy, as we do no recipercate in such customs. Had she cheered we would have returned it. As we passed the upper warehouses I observed my Brother [John W.] and his Satellite John Jackson looking out from the window.[45] Landed as soon as the boat anchored & hastened up home, wishing to avoid acquaintances I took my way up along the "Tombs" & on reaching the house found Sarah awaiting me, having been apprised of my arrival from the counting room. Went round after a little while to see the family. My dear Georgy was standing outside the door on the lookout for me.[46] As ever she was the first to greet me & she did so in all the fullness of her pure heart. How little did either of us then suppose that this was to be my last home welcome from her, & that short days were to shroud her in the tomb. She seemed to have a presentiment of death on my former visit for I well remember her entrusting Capt Farrand as he was leaving the house after dining with us, to return, and before the 20th of June. The request she urged again and again both before and after dinner. He remarked and has mentioned the circumstances. My poor sister was taken sick on Monday and became rapidly worse & worse. Being very much occupied in the duties of the vessel & not dreaming for an instant that it was more than a trifling indisposition I spent very little of my time in her sick chamber for the first two days. On Wednesday morning Diana came out of breath & rousing me from my sleep begged me to hurry to the house, for my poor sister was very ill. I was shocked. I hastened with Sarah & found the whole family assembled round her bedside. The physician had given her up and the poor girl had been told to prepare herself for death, for that there was no hope. Oh my God I could not realize it & stood mute & stupified beside her. She too seemed shocked at the intelligence for her spirit shrunk within her. She became better however in the course of the morning & we fondly hoped that the crisis was passed. On Saturday the 15th of June after tea as I was seated at home reading a comedy, in the full hope that my dearest Georgy was better, Sarah rushed into the room to summon me to her deathbed. Hopes fled from me for the moment & yet as I traversed the dark streets, guided by his lantern I could not but think that my sister would be spared. A sad, sad scene was in store for me. The whole family as on the former occasion were grouped weeping around her. I saw at a glance that she was dying & stood near by to receive her parting breath. Oh how changed she was. Her spirit passed softly away to her God & I leaned close down on her pillow to catch on my cheek her last breath in life. It became fainter & fainter, a slight interval, and with a gentle sigh she had ceased to breath. She was dead. And yet I did not weep. Stern rebellion sprung up in my heart at this my Makers work & looking around upon my relatives I could have asked "Is this the mercy of your boasted God. Can this be for the best. . . . I saw them cut off my sisters hair, lock by lock they clipped it from her & yet I looked on so calm, so tenseless that those around might have thought me heartless. . . . My poor sister was laid out. Her countenance at all time so calm & placid was more beautiful then than I had ever seen it in life. As I stood towards the head of the bed the resemblance to my sister Mary was so striking as to startle me.[47] I could not believe it was Georgia. This was a short time after death. She died at half past ten at night & as it was her desire that she might not be buried until a sufficient time had elapsed to convince all that death had actually taken place, the body was retained until Monday evening at 6 ock, when it was consigned to the grave. The weather being warm, ice & chloride of lime were resorted to, but decay had commenced & showed itself on the ears & throat. The countenance changed towards the last, it became altered in its expression & very yellow. A Mr Stanton was sent for to preserve a likness of her if possible, but he failed in the effort & it was abandoned. I sat up with Georgia the night before she was taken from us, in company with Mrs [Sarah W.] Owens & Dr [Richard] Waynes.[48] Thank God, I was permitted to soothe her closing moments.

On Thursday 26th the family sailed for N.Y. in the Brig Savannah.

June 29th. Left at 4 pm in the steamer Santee to rejoin the Genl Taylor at St Augustine. Reached St Mary's on Sunday night at nine, departed thence at 5 pm & passed into the St Johns a few minutes before 8. At breakfast the boat stopped for a moment to take in passengers. Col Hopkins came on board for a moment & requested me to take charge of a letter for his son.[49] Ran up to Jacksonville. Palatka, Careys ferry at the head of Black Creek &c & arrived at Picolata at half past seven. Took the stage here and reached St Augustine at midnight. Capt Farrand, Lee & Blake met me at the court house corner near the post office. Went immediately on board.

Saturday July 6th. Left the harbour of St Augustine & proceeded to sea, touched at Indian river & landed a live oak agent, two horses & sundry dogs. At 6.30 pm continued our course. Arrived at [the] Miami on Monday 8th at 5.15 pm, remained here wooding until Wednesday 10th. At 6 am of this day got up steam & took our departure at 7 grounded on a ledge, ran out a kedge & hawses on the larboard quarter and attempted to heave her off, failed and shifted the kedge to the larboard bow, at 5.35 pm stood down the bay, passed Key Biscayne, at 7.15 grounded off Soldier Key, got out a kedges, but failed to get afloat again. The musquitos flocked on board at the place in such dense masses that it was almost impossible to breathe without inhaling them, and so venomous were they that although the night was hot to suffocation the officers were obliged to put on pea jackets for protection.

Thursday 11th. At 5.50 am got afloat once more & continued our course down along the reefs. At 7.45 pm anchored off Pine island.

Friday 12th. At 5 am got underway and at 8 am anchored off Key West. Purchased here a new cutter for the vessel and a large English yawl of 3 tons for the captain, towed the latter astern all the way into the Perdido.

Saturday 12th July. At 1 pm a boat from the U S Garrison came alongside with a corporals guard having in charge Jonathan Walker, an abolitionist, turned over by the civil authorities of Key West to be conveyed to Pensacola. Confined him in double irons & placed him below in the Hold.[50]

Sunday 14th at 5.10 am left Key West and stood to the N^{d} W^{d}. Made Egmont Key at daylight on the 15th. 6 am ran through passage Key Pass—passed into the Manatee river and anchored at 8 am 4 miles from its mouth abreast of Col Reids dwelling.[51]

Tuesday 16th at 11.10 Left the Manatee passed out by Egmont at 1.30 and steered W.N.W.

Thursday 18th at sunset arrived in Pensacola Bay and anchored off the Yard.

On the 19th delivered over Jonathan Walker to the city marshall & on the same day furnished Com^{ore} Lavallette with an inventory of all stores, provisions and fuel at present on board the vessel in compliance with his order to that effect. At sundown the Brig [U.S.S.] Lawrence arrived from Havanna.

Thursday 25th. The [U.S.S.] Vandalia arrived and anchored near us.[52]

Sunday 28th at 2.50 am stood out to sea, having been ordered out by Com^{ore} Lavallette. Ran into the Perdido & grounded as soon as we had got into the mouth of the river & were obliged after great labour to remain until the following morning. Weighed kedges, anchores &c & proceeded a short distance when we again struck, got off & struck at a little distance farther up struck again & were obliged to lighten the vessel by passing out chain cables, anchors, water casks etc. What disgusting service for a gentleman to be employed on, to say nothing of carrying abolitionists & cattle. We anchored off the Weehawk Bayou at 4 pm., Perdido. What a place.

> "I'd rather be the thing that crawls
> "Most noxious o'er a dungeons walls
> "Than pass my dull unvarying days
> "Condemned to meditate & gaze
> "On such a waste as this.

Fancy an endless pine barren stretching away on either hand with nought to vary the monotony of the place except the croaking of frogs & chirping of insects. A solitary whip poor will would have been a treasure. I do not object to the woods when within the pale of civilization where one may get his letters and the ordinary comforts of life, but to be enclosed in a fresh water Bayou with the miasma assailing ones nerves as the sun goes down & the heat during the night so intolerable as to leave one enveloped as it were in Gum Arabic is more than my philosophy can bear. Added to this it is impossible to obtain either bread, milk, meat or fruit. During my stay a party of us dug into an Indian mound evidently of great antiquity for on its summit grew a live oak tree of very lofty dimensions, its base measuring not less than from three to three and a half feet in diameter. Around it were other trees of different species also well grown. The mound itself I should suppose to be about 195 feet in circumference. About four feet from the surface we struck a vase & removing the earth carefully from around it discovered that it contained the skull of an Indian with his beads, etc, etc, the bones of the throat we also found but I could not obtain the skeleton of the body. Judging from this I am led to imagine that the head had been severed and so burned for we dug down some distance without find other bones. We excavated in several places & in each threw out quantities of charcoal & fragments of pottery. The vase that I got resembles in shape the upper half of a large pumpkin & is carved with chasing around its border somewhat after the form of a fish, the design evidently having some allusion to one. It covered the face of the corpse, a custom still in vogue I believe among the Florida Indians. Digging in other spots we found other species of pottery and a piece of war paint. The Live Oak on the mound cannot be less than one hundred & fifty years old & contains some of the finest knees, breasthooks &c to be met with anywhere. Thus I passed a Sabbath afternoon. Sunset broke us off from one sacreligious occupation & leaving the fresh earth that we had thrown up, we winded our way back to the boat, blazing trees & breaking twigs as we passed along to find the mound again when inclination led us to farther research there. I must confess that upon reflection, I felt that my time might have been better employed than in disturbing the bones of the dead, it savoured too much of robbing a graveyard & I lay awake in my berth nearly the whole night thinking of death heads & dead Indians. I had placed the skull in an opposite berth & was roused from a fitful sleep by a slight grating noise in the cabin, a mouse had got into the skull and was gnawing the crisp & brittle bones which had lain unmolested perhaps for a century. The idea was poetical at the same time humiliating for little dreamed that proud Indian that his head was to be one day to be wrested from its resting place to be taken to the white mans cabin & there made a nest for the cockroaches & the mouses.

I paid dearly for my yesterdays occupation. My whole body is covered with red bugs & they have buried themselves in my skin beyond the reach of whiskey or cologne. I can neither read, write or sleep. I have been thrown almost into a fever by their incessant itching, my enter body is in lumps & blotches. All the officers who went are suffering in like manner, strange to say the men escaped.

On Monday the 5th experienced the heaviest squall of wind and rain has ever come under my observation. Let go the Larboard anchor, and veered on both chains. It lasted only a few minutes & the sun came out again.

Thursday August 8th. At half past 3 pm of this day left the Weehawk Bayou & felt our way down under easy steam to the mouth of the river. The captain came down later. Manned the cutter & made three very good hauls of the Seine along the sea beach.

Friday 9th At daylight sounded and buoyed the bar, passed out to sea & thence into Pensacola Bay, came to off the Navy Yard & obtained two casks of water. The Vandalia & Lawrence at anchor. Ran up to the Naval Hospital & transferred John Ware & Chas Gill on sick ticket.[53] Proceeded up to Pensacola where we anchored at half past two pm. The Steamer Union, French corvette Brilliante & Brig Mercury off the town. Received a letter from Sarah & sent one by the return mail. I have been very dull of late and have many sad thoughts connected with my late visit to Savannah. My poor sisters [Georgia's] fate comes often among other things to render me gloomy. All her friends are away whilst the poor girl who looked forward with so much pleasure to being along with them now, sleeps alone in the graveyard. Few of us supposed she would die, her life was made up of so much goodness & affection that for her to die before old age came upon her seemed impossible. Her deathbed scene was sublime, she passed so gently away. My Father sobbed like a child, unable to control his feelings. Georgia spoke soothingly to him and said she felt her end was to accomplish some good, perhaps designed especially to bring him to his Savior. My Brother John & myself held the body in our arms until the couch upon which it had lain was smoothed & afterwards placed it in the coffin, a plain silver plate was on the lid & engraved on this her name, "Georgia C. Anderson," nothing more. Nany [Nina] clung convulsively to the coffin & was with difficulty torn from it, she shrieked as it was removed from the room. At the grave an additional scene of sadness awaited us. The sexton in digging out the earth had thrown up and covered the bones of some one of our relatives. I heard also that a piece of a lace cap was also dug up but did not see this latter. In filling up the grave after the coffin had been lowered into it these bones were shovelled in along with fragments of an old coffin &c. I remained till the last & saw the mound heaped up & its sides smoothed off. This then is the end of the sister I loved so dearly, she who had ever been the first to soothe me in my sorrow and espouse my cause in all my little difficulties & trials. We had parted forever, our hopes, our aspirations were at an end & life howsoever bright in future, would still be darkened by the recollection that the sister who started with me in the race was never again to share my prosperity or adversity. Her warm kiss was never to greet me again & the boundless confidence that she had ever been so ready to entrust me with, buried in the narrow grave over which I was bending. Farewell my sister. A few days more & I must mingle among other scenes where I must stifle feeling under a calm exterior & put on cheerfulness when I least feel it, would that I had been a better brother to thee.

Tuesday 13th August. Light breezes with rain. At 2.30 pm left Pensacola and stood up Santa Rosa Bay into the Blackwater river. The object in coming up into fresh water at this season of the year is to enquire into depradations committed upon the pine timber on Government lands in and about this region. The service is gratuitous on the part of Capt Farrand who stakes the lives of his officers and men against paltry pine lumber & that too without a surgeon. This service at any other period would be commendable, but at the present time is both ill judged & improper. The Government neither expect or desire him to cruise in such unhealthy waters, but on the contrary have directed him to remain in Pensacola until further orders. Brought up two passengers. I think we have fed some 30 odd men since I joined the vessel. At 5.45 anchored for a few moments off Bagdad, a collection of mills & dwellings connected therewith, about nine miles from the mouth of the River. Continued up the stream a mile higher and came to off Milltown [Milton].

Wednesday 14th. At 3.30 of this day a party of natives male and female came on board, having been invited off by the captain. As usual he determined to "give them a sail". so weighing anchor we stood up the river about a mile & in returning ran our full length upon a shoal. With logs under the forefoot logs all around us, got out kedges

& hawsers, started water &c &c but to no purpose, we sent the pleasure party back to their homes in the gig & contented ourselves till the next morning when the tide rose & floated us off. The Blackwater is bounded on either bank by fine barrens, the timber of which is not of large growth.

Friday 16th. Left the Blackwater and returned to Pensacola. Two corvettes (french) the U S Steamer Union & brig Lawrence at anchor off the Town.

Monday 19th August at 7.10 am left Pensacola for the Navy Yard, and anchored off there at 7.45. The Vandalia still in her old berth. During our stay at the town six men deserted from the gig of the steamer [U.S.S.] Union taking with them pistols and cutlasses belonging to the vessel and leaving word behind that they would resist any attempt at capture to the death. Thirty dollars reward was immediately offered for each man and a hot pursuit at once instituted by the officers of the vessel and Constables. I have understood that they have all been brought back with the exception of one named Carrol who was shot through the body & killed. There are various stories in circulation as to the manner in which this mans life was taken and therefore I will defer farther comment until I get the right version. Another one of the deserters was shot through the hand. They probably arrived last evening in the Creole from Mobile and are now on board their vessel. These fellows took what is called the Escambia road, leading to the Eastward thinking in this way to baffle pursuit, but sailor like after getting almost into Georgia they retraced their steps by a circuitous route to Mobile and were arrested the moment they arrived there.[54]

On Tuesday 20th for the first time since I joined the boat, all hands were turned up to witness punishment and John Douglass a disrated Quarter Master was whipped with the cats for drunkenness and theft.[55] Capt Farrand arrived just in time to modify his chastisement to 12 lashes for had I been commanding officer a few hours longer I should have given him 20. We are fitting a new cover to the upper deck, and I trust that when it is completed the cabin may be rendered somewhat habitable. For months past we have been drenched with every rain and have been obliged to cover over our bedding with such temporary curtains as would serve to keep out water.

Sunday 25th of Augst. Stormy weather with rain and thunder. At midnight we had a violent storm of wind and rain accompanied by loud thunder and most incessant lightening I have ever before seen. So constant was its flashes that the whole heavens appeared wrapped in flame. The heaviest squalls came from the S^{d} & Westward. I got up several times to look at the weather. Let go the Larboard anchor and veered on both chains. I lay awake in my berth for some time listening to the howling of the storm and watching the lightning as its purple hues were reflected from objects around on the window glass in the forward part of the cabin, the effect was strange and beautiful, but at the same time very solemn. The gale blew itself out by morning and cleared away on Tuesday the 27th, leaving the atmosphere transparent & unclouded, but as cold as November. I found a blanket very comfortable at night. This weather continues up to the present routing, thursday 29th.

We have charming moonlight evenings now. The air is cool clear and bracing. On Tuesday the 27th I strolled on shore with Capt F. and after loitering a moment in Davidsens groggery took the beach & walked to the Hospital, after which we continued on through the woods to the [Fort] Barancas,[56] first having had a glass of champagne & bout of ten pins with Doctor [Isaac] Hulse.[57] Two companies of the [blank] U S Infantry are stationed at the Barancas. They are quartered in huts in the woods, it being considered unhealthy to post them in the adjacent & opposite fortresses. We took tea with Lt [Alexander] & Mrs Montgomery, formerly Matilda Eastin of Pensacola. They live in a small log house & from appearances have but few comforts around them. She was formerly quite a belle among the Naval officers and I have heard it hinted bestowed her affections upon one if not on more of them. She married only a few months since. Lt Montgomery is the officer who lost his 1st wife during the Florida war. She was killed & scalped by the Indians. I think by Coacochee & his band.[58] Soon after tea we took our departure and followed the beach back towards the Navy Yard. The night was heavenly. The moon newly risen was shining brilliantly upon the Bay, the waters of which washed silently the hard beach along which we were treading, whilst the white sand broken here and there by small clumps of brush rendered only more dazzling the moonlight resting upon it. Not the semblance of a cloud or vapour of any kind was to be seen, the sky overhead received a leaden cast from the white contrast below. I thought of home & other scenes, some past, others anticipative. Such evening are calculated to produce reflection.

I see it stated in the papers that a midshipman of the [U.S.S.] Potomac frigate named Bohner had been knocked down & his skull fractured by a mutineer on board of her whilst being confined in irons.[59] The sergeant in attendance very properly cut him down. A Philadelphia newspaper called the American Advocate comes out and attempts to paint a contrast between the "poor sailor loaded with irons in the dark and damp hold of the ship and the luxurious comforts & kind attendance shewn the wounded officer at the hospital." This paper is the organ of the Native American party in Philadelphia most probably of the villianous portion of it, and having such an editor at its head shews I think in pretty fair colours the class of readers for whom the paper is printed. The scoundrel sides of course with the mutineer. I also observe in the public prints of the death of Passed Midshipman [Hamilton F.] Hambleton Porter of yellow fever.[60] He was a shipmate of mine in the Mediterranean Sea and though a very excellent hearted fellow would never have made much of an officer, notwithstanding the newspapers assertion to the contrary. He was too indolent to win in his profession. Glancing my eye over an old Georgian yesterday I saw printed there an extract from a speech delivered in Congress by Mr [Theodore] Frelinghuysen, the Whig Candidate for Vice president of the United States.[61] The extract is given by the Editor with the view of turning votes against him in the State of Georgia. If any one man in my native state can read the paragraph and not think more of Mr Frelinghuysen than he did before he must be devoid of noble sentiments. The following is the extract, it alludes to the removal of the Cherokee indians from the State of Georgia "Let the general Government come out as it should with decided and temperate firmness and officially announce to Georgia and the other States that if the Indian tribes choose to remain they will be protected against all interferences & encroachment * * * This effective weapon the sword, in the hands of our national government, has often been employed to chastise the poor Indians, sometimes with dreadful vengeance I fear, and should not their protection avail to draw it from the scabbard. Let such decided policy go forth now in the majesty of our laws and Georgia will yield. I would rather received the blessing of one poor Cherokee as he casts his last look upon his country, for having though in vain, attempted to prevent his banishment, than to sleep beneath the marble of all the Caesars."

"Thems my Sentiments" Mr Frelinghuysen and they do you credit, provided they came from your heart and were not uttered for your constituents as very many fine things are in Congress. My native state is dear to me & her honor is precious in my eyes as in anybodys, but she did not act well with the Cherokee's.

On Monday the 3d Sept. I received a letter from John Williamson [Sarah's brother] telling me that Sarah was very ill. The intelligence distressed me grievously & almost threw me into a fever from nervousness. This morning 4th, Brother John's letter reached me to say that dear Sarah was better. It grieves me that she should be even indisposed and I not by to comfort her. Capt F left this afternoon for Perdido. I cannot understand how he can bring himself to ask so readily for any indulgence from the hands of a man who has behaved to him like Commodre Lavallette. I should undergo any privation rather than humour such an officer. He came here on separate service and yet submits to a questionable authority in so far as to ask permission to visit his family when if he choses to run up off the town or anchor anywhere but where he now is he would be at liberty to come and go at will. Such humbug would never suit my stomach. We are having a warm spell of weather again, the sea breezes have ceased blowing with their accustomed freshness since the gale of the 20th and there is a smoky vapour hanging over the land in the daytime such as there was in 1839 during the yellow fever season. I trust it may not prognosticate similar results.

Thursday Septbr 5th 1844. The flags of all our vessels in habour have been half masted to day, as also those of the Navy Yard and Naval Hospital in obedience to a general order from the Navy Department, and as a mark of respect to the memory of Commod^{re} A[lexander] J. Dallas who died in Callao Harbour on board the U S frigate Savannah of paralysis. Com^{dre} Dallas was in command of the Pacific squadron. He has been stationed at the yard for many years during his life and appears to have won the esteem of all who knew him here. He is regretted generally and doubtless was a very excellent officer though not perhaps one of the best of the post captains.[62] At meridian thirteen minute guns were fired from the Yard and from the Vandalia. At 3 pm of this day there came up a heavy storm of wind and rain from the N^{d} & E^{d} accompanied with thunder and lightning, the flashes were frightful. The flag staff in the Navy Yard was struck and the conductor shattered. The rain came down so densely as completely to shut out surrounding objects. During the squalls we drifted considerably and as we now lay are a few hundred yards from the Poinsett, we have both anchors ahead with 30 fthms on one chain and about 14 on the other. The breeze has lulled, but appearances are still stormy. During the month of September it blows heavily here from the South East: The bay then has generally a very rough sea running.

Saturday 7th Septbr. I landed about seven pm to vary the monotony of the steamer by a stroll in the yard and a chat with such of the officers as might be at home in their quarters. On passing the sergeants office he handed me a communication from the Navy Dept which on opening I found to be a reply to Capt F's letter requesting information as to the amount of pay I was to receive under my acting appointment. It contained instructions to pay me as passed Midshipman, not as master. This then caps the climax. After nearly ten years of service (indeed full ten) I am to be thrown back upon 750 dollars for annum.

Sunday 8th. Capt F returned this evening from Perdido & I handed him the communication. A court of Enquiry on Capt Lavallette to meet on Monday—.

Monday 9th. Left the yard this morning with a boat load of passengers for Pensacola. Comm^dre^ Lavallette having instructed Capt F to run his vessel as a despatch or passenger boat for the witnesses from day to day during the session of the court of Enquiry. I protested against any such indignity to Capt F, but he views the matter more calmly & suffers it. On arriving at the town I received two letters from JWA [his brother, John], urging in the last one my immediate return to Savannah as my dearest Sarah was lying dangerously ill, packed my trunk immediately and left in the stage at 5 ock for Savannah. My state of mind is too painfully stamped on my memory to need its being chronicled here. Travelled all night & breakfasted the following morning at Halls Tavern after which continued on for a few miles to Halls Landing so called where I took a steamboat for Stockton [Ala.] and so by stage on through Columbus [Ga.] to Macon & thence by railroad to Savannah where I arrived on Saturday evening the 14th. At the 90 mile station I met Mr Benj [E.] Stiles who informed me that Sarah was better & convalescing.[63] The first tidings I had received of her since leaving Pensacola. The recollection of my sufferings on that long and lonely journey recurs now with painful vividness, for I travelled the entire way in ignorance of whether or not I had a wife to greet me on my return & my mind was tortured by a thousand surmises of hope & fear. At Barnesville [Ga.] I looked over the obituary notices in some Savannah papers that I was fortunate enough to borrow there & my hopes revived strongly from this place. Sarah was seated alone in her chamber when I arrived & oh how my heart melted to find her still spared to me. My children were scattered among strangers. Mary [Nina] at the Fannins and Edward at Mrs Mackays. This circumstance brought home desolation to me for although done with the best and purest motives, it shewed me my forlorn position in life and to what my profession subjected me.

About 11 pm I was aroused by the alarm of fire. Mrs Bourkes stable was burning & I hurried over to render such aid as lay within my power.

Sarah relapsed again having taken cold, and suffered much, but gradually regained her health & strength.

17th Septbr. Reported my arrival in Savannah & the circumstances which took me there.

October 4th. Sarah having recovered sufficiently I left Savannah in the cars to rejoin the Genl Taylor at Pensacola. Returned the same evening. 1st Anxiety on Sarah's account, she having shewn so much excitement at parting that I dreaded lest she should relapse again. 2d Having seen a list of the men of war in the harbour of Pensacola, in which the Genl Taylor's name was omitted.

During the earlier part of the month of October (5th & 7th) the coast of the United States & Cuba was swept by a gale which wrecked many vessles & devastated Havanna & the adjoining region. Many lives lost & much property destroyed.

*Saturday Novbr 2*ᵈ Mr Mercer and family arrived at Savannah. Left at 4 pm in the steamer St. Matthews for Picolata & arrived in St Augustine on Tuesday at 2 am, having been detained late on board the boat & also at the landing. Met at Picolata Lt Blake & Jas Williams, bound across the country on a surveying expedition.[64]

Wednesday 6th Dined with Genl Worth & after dinner rode on horseback till sunset. At 9 called at Gen Ws again, he having invited a few gentlemen to meet me.

Friday Nobr 8th My Birthday. I know not whether to rejoice or grieve at the recurrence of this event. It finds me just as poor as ever & with as little prospect of the fullfilment of my anticipations as the last did, yet it comes to me in the flush of health and strength & with hope as boundless as ever. True my heart is not so light nor are my recollections so cloudless as of yore "yet why mourn that such is destiny." Who can tell what the future may have in store for me. Judging from the past I ought not to indulge too sanguinely for my trials have not been retrospective. My error has been to rely too much upon things to come & my vexations have been proportionate. Years are creeping silently along with me & another one if I am spared will take away the last link in the chain of early manhood. How pleasant as a *whole* are the remembrances of my youth and yet I would scarcely live them over again, for there are thorns amidst its roses which pricked too deeply to be easily forgotten and which with my experience of life I should dread to suffer from again. And after all what a sheet anchor is pride to the unfortunate, even though it should be misplaced. How it buoys up the heart in trouble & makes us overlook our own follies in the sense of injury from others, how many a false step it bolsters up & how it incites us to struggle on to the last even when the contest is hopeless. It has its drawbacks too as I can answer for & mars many an opportunity to advancement, as in my own instance. From my rhapsody thus far one would suppose that my sorrows in life had been overwhelming and that the world had dealt harshly with me beyond the ordinary lot of mortals. Tis not altogether so however. My career tis true has been checkered in its windings & the world has sometimes fretted me, yet tis a world very much to my liking and one I would be very well content to continue on in with plenty of money and a light heart to spend it. My grievances are compressed into a narrower limit, the most palpable of which is the sense of poverty when I feel that those who should aid me have it in their power to do so & do not. Every day I find myself more thoroughly convinced of my having been born a gentleman, independently of my father's position in life and that my tactics and feelings would have been the same if I had been born in a horse trough. I must not however begin my birthday by complaining. Let me rather dismiss care and take up with recklessness. My "Log Book" is drawing to a close. It should have been so ere this, for there have been more more trifles connected with my wanderings which might have found a place here with as much profit to myself as those already entered, perhaps with more advantage even, I should like to have chronicled my thoughts & aspirations during the interval since its commencement. I might have established for myself a train of beacons as it were for future government. As it is, the book has served to wile away many a weary moment and to kill *time* which all the while was killing me, stealing away my youth & sapping imperceptibly second by second the buoyant enthusiasm of my life. I would not however if I could, call back again the hopes of my early career as an officer of the Navy. There are moments even now when they flit themselves through me & almost burst my heart with their remembrance. The roll of a drum, the sound of an old song, even the sight of the sea brings back for a moment & only for a moment the thrill which lured me on. And yet it never crossed my mind that I was ambitious, the thing seemed so natural. I thought as a matter of course that every officer felt in the same way. Well well. There doubtless have been other fools as sanguine & probably will be again to the end of time. Let such be my solace.

9th. We had a fine rain yesterday and the streets are pleasant to walk in again. The mail arrived this morning bringing the result of the election in Chatham & Effingham counties Ga. The event produced great exultation among the Democrats & corresponding depression on the part of the Whigs, an odd circumstance when tis remembered that as inhabitants of a Territory they have not the privilege of voting. Visited the old Fort [Matanzas] after dinner & was struck with the strength of the works, their symmetry of construction & the extent of ground covered by them. Viewed from outside the Fort appears small. I was shewn the cell in which Coacochee was imprisoned & from which he effected his escape with some 20 other Indians.[65] The officer who confined him there should have been put there in his stead and made amenable for all the atrocities subsequently committed by him & his band, for a more ready means of escape could not have been offered him. I also saw a secret chamber leading into some dark recesses, the existence of which was made known by accident. The stonework overhead fell in & revealed it & on its being searched with torches, human bones and implements of torture were discovered, whence it is supposed to have been connected with the Inquisition. The door to the chamber in question had been blocked up by the Spaniards prior to the cession to this country, in such a way as to give it the appearance of being part of the adjoining wall and the Americans probably never would have discovered it but for the accidental falling in of the ceiling overhead. The fort is evidently very ancient and I observed on one of the bricks 1703, but as this brick must have been put in at a time when the fort was nearly completed it is evident that the work must be considerably older.

A Sundays wanderings. The day broke clear and beautiful. I hailed its avent as closing a week which had hung heavily on my hands & left me in that most trying of all positions, an uncertainty of purpose arising from the want of definite information to act upon. To pass away time I strolled after breakfast round to the Catholic Church & stood in the doorway listening to the music & criticising the mummery of the priests & their assistants, the little boys who hold the hem of their garments as they figure round about the altar. I noticed several of the U S troops in the church, most probably Irishmen. As soon as the sermon commenced I left the doorway & returned towards the Hotel, passed a procession in the street winding its way towards the church. At its head was a priest & on either side of him two boys bearing wax tapers of extraordinary length & another boy carrying aloft a plated cross. Next came four persons holding at its corners an open coffin in which was a dead child. The eyes were wide staring open & in its little hands was a bunch of fresh flowers which seemed to vibrate stiffly at every step of the bearers. Then came the friends of the deceased walking two by two. They were Minorcans & were going to the church to have mass said over the dead infant & to close its little eyes to all the sins & sorrows of this life, after which the coffin was to be deposited in the grave-yard. Such I was told is the Minorcan custom in St Augustine.[66] Soon after dinner Capt [John T.] Sprague called on me accompanied by a Capt Hannan & we went over the old fort & through its intricacies & dark chambers.[67] A water battery built by the U S Government runs along the Seaward fronts of the fortners adding materially to its strength. From the ditch I noticed the marks of many shots which had buried themselves deeply in the soft substance of which the fort is constructed, and in one place quite an excavation which must have been produced by the planing of several shot in the same spot. These were fired by [Gen. James E.] Oglethorpe. The fortners would soon crumble under the heavy ordnance of the present day. Returning from the works we passed by the Catholic Church & learning that a funeral service was about to be performed curiosity led me to enter & take possession of a vacant pew. Two women were engaged in pinning covers over a couple of tables standing on either side of the altar. They were ugly and old & worked with a business like air very different from what might be expected on so solemn an occasion. After waiting a few moments in the church the funeral procession entered. First came the French priests, then three boys abreast, the middle one carrying the plated cross before mentioned & the two others long wax tapers, next two bodies of adults borne on the shoulders of men & then the relatives & friends of the dead. The coffins were placed on the two biers. The priest aided by a gray headed old man commenced chaunting over the bodies. After this holy water was sprinkled first over the feet, then at the side, next over the head & so on round to the feet again of the coffins. Two little boys going round with the priest & holding either side of his gown. This done the padre takes off his fighting coat with the blazoned cross on the back of it & in a plain white gown burns incense as before over the feet, sides, head &c of the bodies & then the play is ended & the poor souls of the deceased skip into paradise & leave their carcasses behind to be eaten by the worms. I passed out of the church into the street with a smile of contempt on my lips at such woeful ignorance in this enlightened age, but at this instant my eye fell upon a young girl passing in the same direction with myself. She was weeping bitterly & my heart smote me in a moment. I could sympathize deeply in her distress for I had but too recently followed a sister to the grave & what would have been my feelings to have seen a casual looker on smile on that occasion I passed on homewards sadder than I had left it. These poor people live blinded & ignorant as they were by popery & fanaticism possessed at heart warm feelings & pure affections. Doubtless the very mummery which had disgusted me, cheered them with the hope that the dead for whom they mourned had been released from the tortures of purgatory.

The mail from the North & West which was expected in early on Monday evening did not arrive until after breakfast on Tuesday morning. By it I learned indirectly that the steamer still remained in Pensacola. I concluded at once to return to Savannah & the stage being full, Mr Drees procured an open buggy & sent me over to Picolata. Found the steamboat John Stone waiting the arrival of the mail. John Madison on board bound to Savannah. He had with him a pointer puppy which with a little persuasion I induced him to give me. Major Capers & Lady fellow passengers with me.

Thursday 14th Novbr 1844. Arrived in Savannah at 11 A.M. weather damp & chilly & the rain falling heavily, found Nina sick with a very sore mouth & Sarah not very well.[68] The absentees had returned from the North (viz, my Father, Brother George [W]. & Sister [Eliza] Mrs Nicoll).[69] It was upon the occasion of this visit that I came to a formal understanding with my father about leaving the service and planting at Cottonvale. He promises to secure to me all improvements that I may put up on the place so called, with the free use of 20 hands & the profits that may arise from their industry. To give me a certain number of cattle, sheep, two mules, a waggon &c and the use of the house at Lebanon so long as I choose to live in it, or until I am able to build for myself at the other place. He adds a desire for me to have the general superintendance of his own planting interests & a promise of a corresponding proportion of what he may realize from my said superintendence, an indefinite emolument but one that I will cheerfully forego in consideration of the other benefits to be derived from my own property.

Tuesday 19th November. Left at 6 am in the cars and arrived in Macon soon after 6 pm. No passengers by the way but one young man in a state of the most beastly intoxication. Remained one day in Macon to take the Alligator line for Pensacola. Stayed at the Washington Hotel kept by Lanier. After dinner rode round the environs of Macon with a Mr Plant who politely called for me in a vehicle.

Wednesday 20th Novbr at 10 pm commenced my journey for Pensacola. Two fellow passengers inside, a Col Carter and Col Bayley.[70] The roads very good but the route intersected by too many ferries to be agreeable. The eating houses by the way most abominable and filthy, especially at a place called Travellers Rest, on the following Sunday at sunset arrived at the Yellow water river and found the road on the opposite bank completely submerged & impassable for stages or vehicles of any kind. I had the choice now of remaining three days with an uncertain prospect of proceeding at the end of that time in a state, or of risking a wet jacket in crossing the stream & riding 57 miles on an old stage horse during the entire night & a portion of the next day. I decided at once to go on for I felt assured that the anxiety of mind if I did remain would more than counterbalance the bodily fatigue which I should endure in my ride. Accordingly I crossed the ferry, was nearly upset, got wet up to my knees & after much trouble got safely on dry land again. The moon during this time was in eclipse. After riding three miles (I was accompanied by a mail carrier on horseback) we came to a bridge partly washed away & were obliged to dismount & pile the planks up the steep break and then force the horses one by one up the ascent, it was a dangerous experiment & we were detained a long time in accomplishing it. Rode all night long & got a terrible tumble by my horse falling down with me.

Monday 20th at 4 pm arrived at Pensacola & found the Genl Taylor anchored off the wharf. (I left my stage horse at Florida town & crossing the ferry at Escambia river got into a fine stage & went on comfortably.) Captain Farrand was absent when I arrived, having gone some days before to visit his family at Perdido.

On the 27th of November Capt Farrand received a communication from the Navy Dept informing him that the [U.S.S.] Harney had been substituted in the protection of live oak timber, in place of the General Taylor & directing him on her arrival at this port to consider himself detached from this vessel and waiting orders.[71] On the same day I renewed my application for furlough and tendered my resignation from the service in the event of refusal.

Decbr 7th Received the Savannah Republican by this days mail & saw the announcement of poor little Willie Mercers death.[72] Poor dear Nany, how deeply I sympathise with her.

On my last sojourn in Savannah I visited my Sisters Grave. How desolate it looked in its loneliness, for hers was the only grass grown grave there. The rain, the worms & perchance some careless footstep had beaten down the mound from its former proportion and as it stood there in its nakedness with the grass scattered sparsely over it I bent down in silent prayer that Her spirit might hover over me in my wanderings & guard me through all the dangers which may await me in life. That narrow and shrunken mound, so so desolate, lay heaped upon the bosom of one who only a few short months before had sat by my side in the flush of hope & happiness. The kind tone of her voice still rang in my ear her smile, her look, her ladylike demeanor were all fresh in my memory. Four little months ago, she had Being, Form, buoyant health, & now she lay in that lonely grave, cold, pulseless, inanimate. Was she alone in that little enclosure. Oh no. A Mother, three Brothers & a young sister were sleeping beside her & other relatives were there, but long, long years had rolled over *their* interment, and Time had assuaged, if not obliterated the grief which their loss had occasioned. *Hers* was fresh & to me most mournful, for the others had died when I was too young to feel affliction. How strange it seemed that she should be there and those who loved her so, wandering miles, miles away at the North. They have come back since and another little grave has been thrown up near to hers. It has led me to these reflections.

Sunday 22[d] December 1844. Took an early dinner & then bade adieu to the Steamer [*General Taylor*], pulled up to Pensacola in the cutter manned by petty officers & in company with the pilot (Mr Covetter) engaged a room at the Florida house. Received a furlough for six months.

Monday 23[d]. Took the stage at 8 ock am & commenced my homeward journey by the Alligator route. Arrived in Savannah on Saturday evening the 28th.

Tuesday 31st. Left in the stage at 5 am & joined Sarah by dinner time at Mrs Thomas' in McIntosh County. Returned to Savannah on friday 3[d] January 1845. On the 9th reported receipt of furlough & change of residence.

Afterword

ON NOVEMBER 14, 1844, SHORTLY BEFORE HIS DETACHMENT from *General Taylor*, Anderson noted in his diary that he and his father had become somewhat reconciled. If he would quit the Navy, the older man had told him, he would finance him, give him free use of twenty slaves and the family home at Lebanon, and do everything necessary to set him up as a planter. Anderson accepted on a trial basis, took a six months' furlough, and with his family settled down as agreed. However, on May 28, 1845, he sadly noted in his diary that the plan had failed. "The Fates & family jealousy," he added, had dictated differently and his intention to remain at home had quite deteriorated.

One month later, on June 22, he received orders to report to the U.S.S. *Gallatin* at New Bedford, Captain George S. Blake, a small coastal-survey steamer which was engaged in mapping the New England estuaries.[1]

Anderson remained with *Gallatin* for almost a year. But by early 1846, bored with coastal duty and convinced that a war with Mexico was imminent, he requisitioned transfer to combat service. While in New York on May 10 he wrote:

> The City is full of warlike news & excitement & extras are issued from the Newspaper offices some three or four times a day. On the arrival of the intelligence from Texas of the collision between a detachment of our troops and the Mexicans, public feeling seemed roared to an extraor-

> dinary degree. Everybody looked indignant and each face bore marks settled, stern determination. Since then we have confirmation of the first rumors, and we are now at war with the Mexicans. Whether or not it will be pushed as it ought to be I am at a loss to know, but it is to be hoped that no peace will be made with them except at the point of the bayonet. The Navy under Mr. [George] Bancroft will accomplish nothing as I am told he says he has no occasion for the services of the officers. A week or so before the news arrived of the collision he sent in a report to the House saying that the Navy languished from a superfluity of officers & recommending a reduction of one half of this branch of the service. His report has not injured us, but has recoiled on himself as shewing [*sic*] what an impotent inefficient man we have at the head of the department. The papers ridicule him and say he is not qualified for his office either by art education or nature.

Adding that Congress had voted to increase the Army by 50,000 volunteers, he regretted that his old Round Hill teacher "had done nothing as yet in regard to the Navy."

> Yesterday a communication arrived here from Mr. Bancroft to the commander of the Yard, wishing to know how long it would take to fit for sea all the vessels now on the station with the force employed in Nobr. last. The reply was 14 months. The force employed in Nobr. was from 14 to 20 men, and this small number to fit out two frigates, one line of battle ships, four sloops of war and two store ships. Truly Mr. Bancroft had better go back to Boston and write his history.

A week later, back aboard *Gallatin* in Newport, Rhode

Island, he wrote Congressman Thomas Butler King of Georgia, his old family friend, asking his help in securing a transfer to a "fighting ship" in the Gulf of Mexico, in the event "the demonstration by sea against Vera Cruz should [result] in an attack on that place or any movement whatever of a hostile character. . . . I should prefer a frigate if possible as being the class vessel in which most service may be seen," he added, "but if a frigate cannot be had, then a sloop of war will answer me."

Anderson got his wish. He was assigned to the U.S.S. *Mississippi*, a 3,220-ton side-wheel steamer with ten guns, the flagship of Commodore Matthew C. Perry of the West Indian squadron.[2] Within six months Anderson saw action a-plenty: *Mississippi* took part in expeditions against Alvarado, Tampico, Panuco, and the Laguna do los Termimos, all of which were successful in tightening United States control of the Mexican coastline. In January, 1847 *Mississippi* returned to Norfolk for repairs, after which she went back to war, this time leading the amphibious operations against Vera Cruz which was beseiged and captured in March.

While in Norfolk, on February 27, 1847, Anderson received his long-sought promotion to lieutenant. Thus encouraged, he remained in the Navy, despite his earlier bitterness and continued longing for home. But after another unexciting tour of duty with the Coast Survey Department, he resigned, on October 25, 1849, after fifteen years of service, and returned to Savannah.

There he soon became one of Georgia's most distinguished citizens, profitably involved in top-level agricultural, financial, political, and civic affairs. He was twice elected mayor of the City of Savannah before the Confederate War, in 1854 and 1856.[3] He was interested in railroad, steamship, insurance, and real estate businesses, and especially concerned with all activities, on both the local and national levels, which sought to improve coastal navigation, especially in Georgia.

Immediately following the bombardment of Fort Sumter in April, 1861, Anderson was sent to Richmond by Governor Joseph E. Brown to contract with the Tredegar Iron Works for heavy artillery weapons for the State of Georgia. That mission completed, he was summoned to Montgomery by President Jefferson Davis who personally commissioned him a major in the Confederate States Army and ordered him to Europe to purchase ships, arms, ammunition, and other war material.[4]

Upon his successful completion of this seven months' mission, Anderson was promoted to colonel and put in command of the artillery defences of the Georgia coastline, particularly those about Savannah and Brunswick (and later at Charleston), serving under Generals G. T. Beauregard, Lafayette McLaws, and Hugh W. Mercer. In September, 1862 he was entertained in President Davis' home and there offered the post of Assistant Secretary of War. However, after discussing the matter with Secretary George W. Randolph, who frankly declared that he himself was seriously considering resigning the position because the President "constantly interferred" with him personally and "annoyed" him, Anderson respectfully declined the appointment. When Savannah surrendered to General W. Tecumseh Sherman in December, 1864, Anderson was given command of a brigade in General William J. Hardee's corps and appointed commandant of the City of Charleston, South Carolina. Toward the end of the war he was brevetted a brigadier general at Augusta, Georgia.[5]

After the war Anderson returned to civilian life with ever-increasing enthusiasm to reconstruct the South. He was elected Savannah's first post-war mayor in 1865, and was re-elected in 1866, 1867, 1868, 1869, 1873–1874 and 1875–1876, in total making seven terms or eleven years.[6] In addition to being a prosperous planter in association with his nephew, George W. Anderson, Jr.,[7] he was president of the Ocean Steamship Company (which operated nine passenger-freight vessels between Savannah and New York) and a member of the Board of Directors of the Savannah Southern Bank, the Central Railroad of Georgia, the Atlantic and Gulf Railroad, and the Atlantic and Great Western Canal.[8] In 1865 he was elected a member of the Georgia Reconstruction Convention and in 1872 he was summoned to Washington to testify before the joint House-Senate committee investigating conditions in the South.[9]

During these prosperous years Anderson was a frequent visitor to Washington and New York, representing both his own commercial interests and those of Savannah. Always before him was the improvement of navigation and a closer trade relationship between the South and the North. He was twice a guest of President Ulysses S. Grant in the White House,[10] and among his numerous Washington associates were General Sherman, Secretary of the Interior Jacob D. Cox, Secretary of the Treasury George S. Boutwell, Secretary of the Navy George M. Robeson, and Admirals Samuel P. Lee, William B. Shubrick and Daniel Ammen, Senators Alexander H. Stephens, Congressman Joseph E. Johnston, and Captain George Dewey of the Navy Department. In the South his friends included General Robert E. Lee (who was a guest in Anderson's Savannah town house), Georgia's

Governor Joseph E. Brown, Captain John Newland Maffitt, and Generals Robert Toombs and John B. Gordon.

In 1877 Admiral Ammen, who had been a boyhood playmate of President Grant and was a friend of President Rutherford B. Hayes, recommended Anderson to the latter for the position of Secretary of the Navy. Again, in 1881, Ammen, together with General Sherman and other distinguished officials, recommended him for the same post to President James A. Garfield. Obviously, neither recommendation materialized, but they do suggest the high esteem in which Anderson was held, even by those who had a few years before been his enemies.[11]

As his health began to worsen, Anderson, often with his wife and their daughter Sally (born August 5, 1852), would vacation in Saratoga Springs, New York. On May 26, 1880 he complained of "being laid up at home with a severe attack of gout" which had pained him for several weeks. The last entry in his diary, June 24, 1882, states that during a trip to New York he had been "taken with gout & remained sick during the entire visit."

Throughout the summer and fall of 1882 Anderson regained his strength sufficiently to continue his many business activities. In September he attended the christening in Chester, Pennsylvania of *Tallahassee*, the newest vessel of the Ocean Steamship Company, remaining there and in New York for her maiden voyage, arriving in Savannah on October 14.[12]

Exactly a month later, on November 14, the Savannah *Morning News* stated tersely that Edward C. Anderson had been confined to his residence at 87 Charlton Street by a "serious indisposition for the past several days."

On Saturday, January 6, 1883, a cold blustery day, Anderson died quietly, his wife and two sons and two daughters beside his bed. "His friends and family were prepared for the tidings of his death," the editor of the *Morning News* commented on the eighth, "which, from the character of his illness, had been anticipated for weeks past. He was troubled with an affection of the heart, under which he gradually sank and expired the sixty-eighth year of his age."

In the long obituary which followed, his career as a United States naval officer, his service to the Confederacy, and his myriad contributions to Savannah and the South were carefully detailed. A week later the Board of Public Education for the City of Savannah and the County of Chatham, of which Anderson was president, eulogized him as a religious, educational, business, and civic leader. In his passing, the statement concluded, "this community has lost one of its most highly respected and useful citizens, whose name is prominently and honorably connected with many of the most important events in its history."

Anderson's funeral services were conducted by the Reverend Doctor L.S.K. Axson in the Independent Presbyterian Church with which the deceased had been affiliated since boyhood. And his remains were interred in the Anderson Family Plot at Laurel Grove Cemetery. "The floral tributes were numerous and beautiful," declared the *News*, particularly the one so appropriately designed and placed on his grave by the Ocean Steamship Company—"a large model of a full-rigged ship made of immortelles and roses."[13]

Notes

Foreword

1. For permission to use the Anderson Papers, both those on loan to the University of North Carolina Library and in the Schwalb Collection (photocopies in The University of Alabama Library), and for her gracious assistance, the writer is indebted to Mrs. J. Fred (née Florence Crane) Schwalb, Anderson's great-granddaughter, 121 E. Gwinnett St., Savannah. Among the many items in these collections is a seven-volume diary, or journal, kept by Anderson, covering the years Feb. 8, 1842–June 26, 1846, 1861–1864, and 1869–1882. The 1861–1862 diary, edited by the writer as *Confederate Foreign Agent: The European Diary of Major Edward C. Anderson*, was issued in 1976 by the Confederate Publishing Co., University, Ala.
2. Throughout his diaries Anderson frequently reminisces about home and family, often expressing opinions about people and past events. For example, the comments quoted here about his father, mother, and boyhood were written Sept. 12, 1843, several years after he had joined the United States Navy.
3. George Anderson and Debrah (Grant) Anderson of New York City (Edward's grandparents) were married in 1763 and moved to Savannah shortly thereafter. He was owner of *Georgia Pacquet* which plied between Savannah and England. The father of three children (George, Jr., John, and Mary), he was lost at sea in Sept., 1775 (Anderson Genealogy, Schwalb Collection; Robert M. Myers, ed., *The Children of Pride* . . . [New Haven, 1973], 1452).
4. *Dictionary of American Biography* (New York, 1928+), I, 564–70 (Bancroft); IV, 273–74 (Cogswell), hereinafter *DAB*.
5. Northampton *Gazette*, Oct. 8, 1823; May 27, 1830 and *passim*.

6. Anderson's name leads the list of eighteen Round Hill scholars from Georgia in *Names of Pupils of Round Hill School, Northampton, Mass., from Its Commencement Until June, 1831* (Newport, R. I., 1862). The careers of Forbes and Motley are in *DAB*, VI, 507–08 and XII, 282–86.
7. Eliza Williamson of Savannah, sister of Sarah, Anderson's wife-to-be, attended Ghuerardi's school, 1826–1827 (letters, Nancy Read of Savannah to Eliza at Northampton, Aug. 23, Oct. 1, 1826, and May 29, 1827, Schwalb Collection).
8. M. A. DeWolfe Howe, *Life and Letters of George Bancroft* (New York, 1908) II, 168ff. Bancroft (1800–1891) was defeated as the Democratic candidate for governor of Massachusetts in 1844, but was appointed Secretary of the Navy by President James K. Polk. In 1846–1849 he was ambassador to Great Britain and in 1867 minister to Germany. The last volume of his history was completed in 1876 (*DAB*, I, 564–70).
9. Upon leaving Round Hill, Cogswell (1766–1871) became headmaster of a school in Raleigh, N. C. In 1840 he joined the staff of the New York Public Library and from then until 1861 he devoted his time to building the John Jacob Astor Collection (ibid., IV, 273; Anna Eliot Ticknor, ed., *The Life of Jos. G. Cogswell as Sketched in His Letters* [Boston, 1874]).
10. *Prospectus of a School To Be Established at Round Hill, Northampton* . . . (Cambridge, 1823); *Some Account of the School for Liberal Education of Boys Established at Round Hill* . . . (Northampton, 1826); and *Outline of the System of Education at Round Hill School* . . . (Boston, 1831). The institution is described in "The School at Northampton," *United States Literary Gazette*, I, 331–32 (Feb. 15, 1825) and George E. Ellis, "Recollections of Round Hill School," *Educational Review*, I, 337–44 (Apr., 1891).
11. On his twenty-ninth birthday Anderson again referred to his unhappy boyhood and the "thorns" of his youth (see above, n. 2 and Diary, Nov. 8, 1844).
12. Woodbury (1789–1851) was Secretary of the Treasury and Secretary of the Navy under President Andrew Jackson (*DAB*, XX, 488–89). It is not unreasonable to suppose that Anderson

received Bancroft's support in obtaining this appointment.

13. "A Statement of the Services of Passed Mids Edward C. Anderson from the Time of His Entrance (or First Appointment) to the 31st December, 1841" in "Returns of Services of Officers, 1825–1842" (Office of Naval Records and Library, National Archives, Washington, D. C. [hereinafter ONRL]). This manuscript volume, the only one of its kind prior to the Confederate War, gives in detail Anderson's record from Oct. 20, 1833 to Dec. 8, 1841. Additional information is in Thomas H. S. Hamersly, comp., *Complete General Navy Register of the United States from 1776 to 1887* (Washington, 1888), 28.

14. The log of *St. Louis*, as well as those of *Grampus*, *Falmouth*, *Lexington*, *Macedonian*, *Mississippi*, *Porpoise*, *Warren*, *Vandalia*, and others which featured in Anderson's career, are in ONRL.

15. Anderson's certificate of appointment, signed by President Jackson and Secretary of the Navy Mahlon Dickerson, is in the Schwalb Collection, and his letter of acceptance, written "At Sea, Feb. 1, 1837" aboard the U.S.S. *Constitution*, is in ONRL.

16. *DAB*, VI, 96–97; Hamersly, 234; and Allan Westcott, "Commodore Jesse D. Elliott, A Stormy Petrel of the Navy," *United States Naval Institute Proceedings*, LIV, 773–78 (Sept., 1928).

17. Cass (1782–1866) was Secretary of War under President Jackson, 1831–1835, minister to France, 1836–1842, senator from Michigan, 1845–1851, the Democratic Party's nominee for President, 1844, 1848, and 1852, and President James Buchanan's Secretary of State, 1856–1860 (*DAB*, III, 562–64).

18. Anderson's journal, kept during his trip through the Holy Land, edited by this writer, may be seen in *Journal of the American Oriental Society*, XCV, 633–44 (Oct.–Dec., 1975).

19. *DAB*, XVII, 136–37; Hamersly, 647. Shubrick (1790–1874) retired as rear admiral in 1861. He and Daniel Ammen (see below, n. 26) were Anderson's lifelong friends (see Afterword, n. 11).

20. Histories of *Constitution*, *Falmouth*, *Lexington*, and *Macedonian* are in *Dictionary of American Naval Fighting Ships* (Washington, 1959+), II, 174, 387–88; III, 60; IV, 101–02, 179–80 (hereinafter *DANFS*). Of this work only five volumes (A–Q) have been published (1974).
21. Anderson's certificate of promotion, signed by President Martin Van Buren and Secretary of the Navy James K. Paulding, July 16, 1840, is in the Schwalb Collection.
22. Although christened Mary, Jan. 12, 1845, she was called "Nina." The name has since passed from one generation to another. Perhaps the best known was Anderson's granddaughter, Nina Anderson Pape (1869–1944), one of Georgia's most beloved and respected educational and civic leaders. She worked with Juliette Low in establishing the Girl Scouts of America (Savannah *Morning News* and Savannah *Evening Press*, March 6, 1944, and Diary, n. 14). Edward Maffitt served on the C.S.S. *Alabama*, 1862–1864 (Arthur Sinclair, *Two Years on the Alabama* [Boston, 1895], 319–21; W. Stanley Hoole, ed., "Letters from a Georgia Midshipman on the C.S.S. *Alabama*," *Georgia Historical Quarterly*, LIX, 416–32 [Winter, 1975]).
23. On May 12, 14, 24, 1842, while *Falmouth* was in Brooklyn, Anderson submitted his resignation to Secretary of the Navy Abel P. Upshur (see below, n. 27), but by the time the papers cleared he had decided to remain in the Navy. This incomplete and enigmatical exchange of correspondence (in ONRL) fails to reveal the reasons behind Anderson's vacillation. He does not clarify the matter in his diary.
24. Lebanon and the other Anderson plantations (Berwick, Cottonvale, and Saranac) were in Chatham County, about ten miles northwest of Savannah, between the Little Ogeechee River and Salt Creek. The family home at Lebanon (since 1804), which had fallen into very bad condition following the Confederate War, was recently restored by Dr. and Mrs. Howard J. Morrison, 26 E. Gaston St., Savannah (see Afterword, n. 7).
25. *DANSF*, II, 329.

26. *DAB*, I, 258–59; Hamersly, 27. Ammen (1819–1898) retired in 1878 as rear admiral. During the Confederate War, as captain of the U. S. S. *Patapsco*, he participated in the siege of Savannah by bombarding Ft. McAllister which was under Colonel Anderson's command. After the war the two men were close friends (see above, n. 19 and Afterword, n. 11).
27. Hamersly, 628 (Sands), 727 (Upshur). Sands became a midshipman in 1812 and retired as rear admiral in 1866.
28. Anderson's "*back date*" reference concerns an error in the date of his enlistment. He joined in 1833, but the record book mistakenly showed 1834, thus setting him back in the list of promotions. Throughout these months he wrote several letters (in ONRL) to Justice Wayne and to Congressman Thomas Butler King, of Georgia, asking their help (*DAB*, 565–66 and X, 403; see Diary, n. 2).
29. *DANFS*, IV, 101–02. Anderson's friend Shubrick (see above, n. 19) was *Lexington's* first commander when she was launched in 1826.
30. On May 7 Anderson noted in his diary that he had received a "gratifying" answer to his letter, but he did not incorporate it in his diary.
31. Hamersly, 391; *DAB*, X, 164–65. Jones, a Virginian, enlisted in 1836, was promoted to lieutenant in 1849, and resigned in 1861 to become a captain in the C. S. Navy.
32. Obviously named for Zachary Taylor, this little vessel was purchased by the Navy in 1840 (*DANFS*, III, 60–61).

Diary

1. Farrand, a Floridian, resigned, Jan. 21, 1861 to join the C. S. Navy (Hamersly, 244). At the Battle of Drewry's Bluff, May 15, 1862, he won congratulations from Congress for his "gallantry, courage and endurement" (J. Thomas Scharf, *History of the Confederate States Navy* . . . [New York, 1881], and 717 and *passim*).
2. The Dubignon family owned Jekyll Island, according to

Tom Henderson Wells, *The Slave Ship Wanderer* (Athens, 1967), 25 ff., but Charles is not mentioned. King (1800–1864), a native of Massachusetts, moved to Georgia in 1822. He served five times in Congress in the 1830's and 1840's, becoming chairman of the Committee on Naval Affairs. In 1861, as a Confederate commissioner to Europe, he attempted but failed to establish steamship connections between the South and England, Belgium, and France (*DAB*, X, 403).

3. See Albert C. Manucy, *The Fort at Frederica* (Tallahassee, 1962). Oglethorpe (1696–1785) was the founder of Georgia (*DAB*, XIV, 1–3).

4. Jacksonville, the ninth town in Florida Territory to be incorporated, was a stronghold for refugees during the Seminole Wars. In 1840 there were less than six hundred inhabitants in the community, but trade with Savannah was increasing and commerce was beginning to flourish (Sidney W. Martin, *Florida During the Territorial Days* [Athens, 1944], 188–89; T. Frederick Davis, *History of Jacksonville, Florida and Vicinity, 1513–1924* [St. Augustine, 1925], 293; and W. Stanley Hoole, ed., "East Florida in 1834," *Florida Historical Quarterly*, LII, 294–308 [Jan., 1974]).

5. Picolata, a boat-landing for liveoak timber cutters, had been an Army supply depot and base hospital during the Seminole Wars, but by 1844, as Anderson states, it had all but dwindled away (ibid., 190; John K. Mahon, *History of the Second Seminole War* [Gainesville, 1967], 279).

6. Williams was a justice of the peace for St. John's County in 1835 and a signer of a petition to Congress, Apr. 22, 1840, seeking separate statehood for East Florida (Clarence E. Carter, ed., *Territorial Papers of the United States: The Territory of Florida, 1839–1845* [Washington, 1956–1962], XXV, 105; XXVI, 136, 270, 316). He was author of *The Territory of Florida* . . . (see below, n. 12).

7. *St. Matthews* was a steam-packet that plied regularly between Savannah and Palatka, according to Joseph Bancroft, *Census of the City of Savannah* . . . (Savannah, 1848), 31.

8. Thistle had commanded a company under Maj.-Gen. Edmund P. Gaines in the Seminole Wars. He was at this time serving as a government "live oak agent" (John T. Sprague, *Origin, Progress, and Conclusion of the Florida War . . .* [New York, 1848], 109). See also Carter, XXVI, index, and Diary, Apr. 6, 7, May 29, 1844.
9. Palatka, like Picolata, was a small trading post in the 1830's that became an important military depot during the Seminole Wars. A large hospital, stables, barracks, and eight blockhouses were erected there in 1840. After the wars it declined in prominence (Martin, 190; Mahon, 263ff.).
10. Carter, XXVI, 138, 607, 977, lists four Pecks—Fenn, John E., Samuel H., and S. T. Evidence suggests the pilot to have been Fenn Peck who was a signer of a petition to Congress in Palatka, Jan. 26, 1843.
11. Ibid., XXVI, 83, 502–03, records Stephen and Lewis Grimes, both of whom were signers of a petition praying the admission of Florida Territory as a state, Aug. 13, 1842.
12. Fort Mellon was named for Capt. Charles Mellon, 2nd Artillery, who in 1835 had been ordered to protect the family of the late Charles O'Matler from Indian "villiany" (ibid., XXV, 200; John Lee Williams, *The Territory of Florida . . .* [New York, 1837], 221, 268 [view]).
13. Carter, XXVI, 470, 480, 613, 688 mentions a "Major —— Taylor" and his unsavory litigations regarding timber land settlements.
14. Nany was Anderson's daughter Mary, called Nina (see Foreword, n. 22 and below, n. 68).
15. Carter, XXVI, 737, records Brush as a signer of a petition to Congress for a road between St. Augustine and Palatka, and Williams (57) mentions him as having come to Florida from New York.
16. Holland had been recommended by Thistle to Secretary of the Treasury John C. Spencer for the position of customs collector of East Florida, June 29, 1843 (Carter, XXVI, 674;

DAB, V, 166–67; W. Stanley Hoole, *Four Years in the Confederate Navy* . . . [Athens, 1964], 8 ff.). Sadler, a planter, was the husband of Catherine, daughter of John Houstoun McIntosh (Myers, 1668–69).

17. Worth (1794–1849) was brevetted brigadier-general on March 1, 1842 for gallant service in the Seminole Wars and promoted to major-general during the Mexican War (W. H. Powell, *List of Officers in the United States Army from 1779–1900* [New York, 1900], 690). See also, Mahon, Sprague, *passim*, and below, n. 39.

18. Later, in November, Anderson re-visited Fort Matanzas which had been built in 1672–1695 (see below, n. 66). His drawing of the fort may be interestingly compared with more recent photographs of it in Charles B. Reynolds, *Old St. Augustine* (St. Augustine, 1885), 51, and Henry G. Cutler, *History of Florida Past and Present* (Chicago, 1923), I, 28.

19. William A. Read, *Florida Place-Names of Indian Origin and Seminole Personal Names* (Baton Rouge, 1934), 73, describes Coacoochee ("Wild Cat") as "probably the most dangerous of all Seminole chiefs. . . . With a band of eighty warriors he overran the country lying between St. Augustine and the head of the St. Johns River." See also, Joshua R. Giddings, *The Exiles of Florida* . . . (Columbus, 1858), 176 and below, n. 65.

20. St. Augustine, an important military base, was also a health resort and a fruit, agricultural, and shipping center. In 1840 only one-half of its 2,000 population was strictly American, the others being Spanish, French, Creeks, and Italians (Martin, 184; Mahon, 131–32).

21. Blake and Lee were officers in the 8th Infantry, under Worth (Francis B. Heitman, *Historical Register and Dictionary of the United States Army . . . 1789 to March, 1903* [Washington, 1903], I, 223, 623; see below, n. 28).

22. It is odd that Anderson does not mention Fort Dallas, named for Comdr. Alexander J. Dallas, which stood near the mouth of the Miami River, opposite Key Biscayne. Built in

1838, it was abandoned in the 1850's. The site is now within the limits of Metropolitan Miami (Sprague, 223–24; Read, 17; below, n. 41, 62). A photograph of one of the buildings appears in Cutler, I, 396.

23. Spelled *coontie* and *kunti*, this tropical plant of the cycad family has large dark green feathery leaves, resembling ferns or palms. As Anderson observed, the underground roots yield a starch-like flour, highly valued by the Seminoles. See also, Martin, 117 and below, n. 40.

24. Key West, which had been an important naval base since 1822, was a flourishing but almost lawless community with wharves, warehouses, two newspapers and many fine homes in 1844 (Martin, 195–96). For a view of the place in the 1830's see Rembert W. Patrick, *Florida Under Five Flags* (Gainesville, 1945), 41. Carter, XXVI, 665–66, contains a note from Worth to Army headquarters in Washington, June 19, 1843, stating his intention to visit Key West.

25. Merchant, from New Hampshire, was a lieutenant in the 8th Infantry (Heitman, I, 703) and the 197-ton *Philura*, Capt. [?] Thatcher, was a regularly scheduled packet between Savannah and New York (Bancroft, 30).

26. Marvin, from New York State, was appointed U. S. attorney for South Florida by President Jackson in 1836 (Carter, XXV, 224–25).

27. Fort Brooke, named for Col. George M. Brooke, sometime commander at Tampa, was built in the 1820's and in the 1840's was headquarters for the Army in Florida (Sprague, 52 ff. and *passim;* Heitman, I, 248). During the wars 3,000 troops were stationed there, but by 1845 it was virtually deserted (Martin, 238). The site is now within the limits of Tampa (Cutler, I, 313).

28. Lee was appointed lieutenant in 1838. He was brevetted lieutenant colonel in 1863, retired in 1866, and died in 1879 (Powell, 429).

29. In Daniel Haskel and J. Calvin Smith, *A Complete Descriptive*

and Statistical Gazetteer of the United States . . . (New York, 1844), 648, and William Chapin, *A Complete Reference Gazetteer of the United States of North America* (New York, 1843), 304, Tampa is tersely mentioned as the "p.o., Hillsborough County," but considerable space is devoted to Tampa Bay as "the largest bay in the Gulf of Mexico" and "important as the headquarters of the operations against the Seminole Indians." There is a view of Tampa village at this time in Sprague, 287.

30. Scriven and Belknap were officers in the 5th and 8th Infantry (Heitman, I, 207, 870; Sprague, 554).

31. Sampson, a slave belonging to Col. Gad Humphreys, was captured by the Indians in 1837 and held two years (ibid., 315–19).

32. See Kenneth W. Porter, "Billy Bowlegs (Holata Micco) in the Seminole Wars," *Florida Historical Quarterly*, XLV, 219–42 (Jan., 1967).

33. St. Joseph, thirty miles southeast of Panama City, was settled about 1830 and was the site of the first Florida constitutional convention in 1838. Today it is virtually non-existent (Cutler, I, 118).

34. Carter, XXVI, 423–24, quotes a letter from Gabriel J. Floyd to Rep. David Levy, Apalachicola, Jan. 21, 1842 in which "Dr. ______ Price" is described as seeking "influence in favour of geting [*sic*] Saint Joseph made a separate Port of entry."

35. Pensacola had been an American naval base for twenty-three years in 1844 and was a thriving community of 2,000 people (Martin, 170; Haskel and Smith, 521).

36. *Poinsett*, a 250-ton side-wheel gunboat, after serving in the Seminole Wars, had been assigned to coastal survey duty, mostly in the Tampa area (*DANFS*, V, 337). LaVellette was retired as rear admiral in 1862 (Hamersly, 421). *Brilliante* remained at Pensacola until Sept. 18, 1844 (Pensacola *Gazette*, Sept. 21, 1844).

37. Perdido River and Bay form the boundary between West Florida and the State of Alabama (Chapin, 243).

38. Gerry, who had become a commander in 1842, was lost in the U.S.S. *Albany*, Sept, 28, 1854 (Hamersly, 278).
39. Sprague, aide-de-camp to Worth, 8th Infantry, was the author of *Origin, Progress, and Conculsion of the Florida War* . . . (see below, n. 58; Heitman, I, 913).
40. English was illegally appointed to the Legislative Council of Florida, Southern District, by the Executive Department, Tallahassee, March 3, 1841, and was soon replaced by J. B. Brown (Carter, XXVI, 275). From his mother, Harriett English, sister of Col. F. F. Fitzpatrick of South Carolina, English inherited the land that is now the City of Miami. He moved there in 1844 with his slaves, put the plantation property back in order (it had been damaged by U. S. troops), and set about to establish a town. However, he left for California in 1850 to find gold in order "to build a city," failed, returned, and in 1855 accidentally shot and killed himself (Cutler, I, 394–95).
41. Anderson's prediction that the Miami River region would never be "much more" than it was in 1844 is in sharp contrast to that of English who was "sanguine of establishing a flourishing settlement" there and had already "laid out a town &c yet to be built" (see above, n. 22 and below, n. 62).
42. Probably Fort Ann, near the Haulover which separated Mosquito Lagoon from Indian River (Carter, XXVI, 780, 831, 1023).
43. Formerly a receiver in the St. Augustine Land Office, Cole was involved in many real estate transfers (ibid., XXVI, 55ff.).
44. Van Ness was paymaster for the 8th Infantry (Heitman, I, 983; Sprague, 523). Capers is not listed in Heitman or Powell, but Carter, XXVI, 274 ff., identifies him as a "dispursing agent" at Tampa in 1841 and cites his various transactions.
45. John Wayne Anderson (1805–1866), who married Sarah A. Houstoun (1814–1868), was the second son of George and Eliza Clifford (Wayne) Anderson, the first being George W. (1796–1872), who married Elizabeth C. Stites (1805–1865), and the third being Edward, himself. Two other boys, Richard and

James, died in infancy (see Foreword, n. 3; below, n. 69; Myers, 1453).

46. Georgia Ann (b. 1812 [?]), Edward's favorite sister, died within ten days after this greeting, on June 15, as will be noted. He grieved over her death, frequently referring to her in his diary (see, for instance, Aug. 9, Dec. 7, 1844).

47. Mary Stites Anderson, dates unknown, became the wife of Gen. Hugh W. Mercer, C.S.A. (see below, n. 72; Myers, 1623; Alexander A. Lawrence, *A Present for Mr. Lincoln . . .* [Macon, 1961], *passim*).

48. Myers, 1638, 1718–1719. Mrs. Owens was the wife of George S. Owens, a lawyer and planter, and Dr. Wayne, a graduate of Union College, Schenectady, N. Y., was six times the mayor of the City of Savannah.

49. Heitman does not list Hopkins, but Carter (XXIV, 1149) names an L. A. Hopkins who was associated with John Allmand in the liveoak cutting business.

50. Walker (1799–1878), a native of Massachusetts and a former sea captain, became a railroad contractor in Florida in 1840. He aided several Negro slaves to escape to the West Indies in 1844. Captured, he was imprisoned in Pensacola (chained to the floor), convicted by a U. S. court, pilloried and branded on his hand with the letters "S.S." ("Slave Stealer"). He was the subject of John G. Whittier's poem, "The Man with the Branded Hand" (*Appleton's Cyclopedia of American Biography* [New York, 1889], VI, 328). The story is detailed in Pensacola *Gazette*, June 29, 1844, and mentioned in Carter, XXVI, 934–35.

51. Unless this was Col. Robert R. Reid, governor of Florida in 1839–1840, he must remain unidentified (Mahon, 263ff.; Cutler, I, 118; and Carter, XXVI, 1191–93).

52. The 364-ton *Lawrence* was launched at Baltimore, Aug. 1, 1843 (*DANFS*, IV, 68). *Vandalia*, is not in *DANFS*, but see Foreword, n. 14.

53. Ware and Gill were seamen on *General Taylor* (see Diary, above, p. 14).

54. *Union*, "one of the wonders of the day" because of its submerged propellor, was visited by many sightseers during her stay in Pensacola (Pensacola *Gazette*, June 29, 1844). The story of the desertion of the six sailors from *Union* is recorded in the New Orleans *Picayune*, copied from the *Gazette*, Sept. 3, Oct. 10, Nov. 19, 1844. *Union* remained in Pensacola until fall, at which time she departed for Vera Cruz (ibid., Sept. 28, 1844).

55. Douglas is not listed as a member of the crew of *General Taylor* (see above, Diary, pp. 13–14), but a quartermaster named Oliver Carpenter and Seamen Henry Burns and Samuel Green were recorded by Anderson as having jumped ship at Blackwater in December, 1844.

56. Barrancas, on the mainland southwest of Pensacola, had been the site of a fort since the late 1690's when the Spaniards erected Fort San Carlos. At the beginning of the Confederate War, Barrancas was occupied by Southern troops, but within a year the entire Pensacola Bay area was in the hands of the Federals (Cutler, I, 363, 367).

57. Hulse was a Navy surgeon (Hamersly, 368).

58. The massacre of the first Mrs. Montgomery, wife of Lt. Alexander Montgomery, 7th Infantry, on Dec. 28, 1840 was one of the most brutal episodes in the Seminole Wars. Escorted by Lts. Walter Sherwood and N. Hopson, Sgt.-Maj. Carrol, and ten privates, Mrs. Montgomery was moving from Micanopy to Watkahoota (eight miles), accompanied by a wagon and five mules. They were ambushed by thirty Indians, led by Halleck-Tustenuggee and Cosa-Tustenuggee. Mrs. Montgomery was killed instantly, a panic ensued, and Hopson was sent back to Micanopy for help. Sherwood, Carroll, and Pri. Lansing Burlingham, and perhaps others, were killed and their bodies mutilated. Cosa-Tustenuggee and his warriors were captured near Palaklikaha, imprisoned at Fort King, and in June, 1841 were sent, with their families, to Arkansas (Sprague, 249–50, 484–85). "The infamy of his own acts," Sprague stated, "acci-

dent, and the resolution of the detachment of dragoons . . . had relieved Florida of an Indian chieftain, cruel, cowardly, and vindictive." See also, Carter, XXVI, 898, Mahon, 284; Giddings, 278, and George R. Fairbanks, *History of Florida* . . . (Philadelphia, 1871, 325–26).

59. *Potomac,* 726 tons, was launched in 1822. She patrolled the Gulf of Mexico and Carribbean in 1847 and participated in the seige of Vera Cruz (*DANFS*, V, 363).

60. Hamersly, 575. Porter enlisted Apr. 12, 1836, became passed midshipman July 1, 1842, and died Aug. 10, 1842.

61. Frelinghuysen (1787–1862), of New Jersey, was Henry Clay's running mate on the Whig ticket. They lost to James K. Polk and Richard M. Johnson (*DAB*, VII, 16–17; X, 115; XV, 34–38).

62. Dallas was the son of the Secretary of the Treasury under President James Madison and brother of Vice President George M. Dallas (ibid., X, 38–39). He planned Pensacola Navy Yard in the early 1830's, prior to taking command of the West Indian Squadron (Rossiter Johnson, ed., *Twentieth Century Biographical Dictionary of Notable Americans* . . . [Boston, 1909], III, n. p.). See also, Hamersly, 188; above, n. 22, 41; and Pensacola *Gazette*, Sept. 7, 1844.

63. Stiles was a wealthy planter who married Mary A. Mackay (Myers, 1609, 1689).

64. Probably Lt. James S. Williams, a Georgian, who had in 1837 resigned from the Army (Heitman, 1041).

65. See above, n. 18. Coacooche (Wildcat), one of the most daring and intelligent of Seminole chiefs, was captured and imprisoned in St. Augustine in 1841. He escaped, was recaptured and eventually sent to Arkansas (Sprague, 271, 329, and *passim;* Carter, I, XXVI, 276ff.; above, n. 19).

66. A colony of 1,500 Roman Catholic Minorcans, from the island in the Mediterranean Sea, settled in the vicinity of New Smyrna in 1768 (Reynolds, 83–90; Martin, 198–99).

67. Carter, XXVI, 269, 494, 604, lists a John Hannan and E. W. Hannon, both signers of petitions concerning land surveys and Indian affairs.
68. In earlier references Anderson called her Nany (see above, n. 14).
69. George married Elizabeth C. Stites and their son was Edward Clifford Anderson II. Eliza was the wife of Judge John C. Nicoll, District Court, Eastern Circuit of Georgia, 1839–1861 (Warren Grice, *The Georgia Bench and Bar* [Macon, 1931], 108, 352, 375; Warren Grice, "The Confederate States Court for Georgia," *Georgia Historical Quarterly*, IX, 131–58 [June, 1925]).
70. Carter, 44 ff. lists a Lt. Col. William J. Bailey, who was also a territorial adjutant and inspector general, and several Carters, none a colonel. Neither is mentioned in Hamersly.
71. *Harney* was named for Lt. Col. William S. Harney who had served with distinction in the Seminole Wars (Powell, 357; Mahon, 260ff). See also, Pensacola *Gazette*, Feb. 1, 1845.
72. Little Willie (William Gordon) Mercer, the son of Hugh and Mary Stites Anderson Mercer (see above, n. 47), was born *c.* 1840 and was therefore about the same age of his cousin Nina.

Afterword

1. *Gallatin* is not in *DANFS*. Blake, who had enlisted in 1818, became commodore in 1862, and died in 1871 (Hamersly, 75). One of Anderson's shipmates on *Gallatin* was John Newland Maffitt who later won fame as captain of the C.S.S. *Florida* (ibid., 451; Scharf, 790).
2. *Mississippi* was launched in 1842. She assisted in the capture of New Orleans, but was sunk by the Confederates off Port Hudson, March 14, 1862 (*DANFS*, IV, 387–388; Hamersly, 562).
3. William Harden, *A History of Savannah and South Georgia* (Chicago, 1913), I, 450–52.

4. *ORA*, 1, I, 318–20 and 1, LI (2), 221 ff. Anderson returned to Savannah on the C.S.S. *Fingal*, Nov. 12, 1861, bringing in supplies valued at $250,000, the largest shipment of rifles, sabres, cannon, gumpowder and medical supplies ever to reach the Confederacy in a single bottom (Hoole, *Four Years in the Confederate Navy . . . , 5–22).*

5. Savannah *Daily News and Herald*, Aug. 31, 1868.

6. Harden, I, 482–83.

7. In 1873 the Andersons transported seven families from France to Lebanon to experiment with the cultivation of grapes and wheat. This settlement, known as L'Esperance, is reminiscent of the short-lived "Vine and Olive Colony" established in Alabama by refugees from France in 1817 (Savannah *Morning News*, Apr. 23, 1873; Albert B. Moore, *History of Alabama* [University of Ala., 1934], 78–79).

8. In addition, Anderson was president of the Board of Public Education for the City of Savannah and County of Chatham, and a member of the governing bodies of Chatham Academy, the Georgia Historical Society, Massie School, the Georgia Infirmary, the Savannah Hospital for Negroes, the Savannah Port Society, the Chamber of Commerce, and the Independent Presbyterian Church.

9. *Testimony Taken by the Joint Select Committee to Inquire Into the Condition of Affairs in the Late Insurrectionary States: The Ku Klux Conspiracy* (Washington, 1872), VI, 175–82.

10. Anderson wrote that Grant "struck me as an unostentatious man, but at the same time one whose grasp of intellect was by no means up to the high position of statesmanship required in the office. . . . I must do Genl Grant however the justice to say that he met me very courteously and with apparent cordiality . . . devoting himself exclusively to me during the entire evening" (Diary, Jan. 23, 1870).

11. Ibid., Feb. 23, 1877 and June 11, 1881. Sherman and Ammen had both shared in the siege and capture of Savannah in December, 1864 (see above, Foreword, n. 26).

12. *Tallahassee*, a 2,100-ton steamer, 315 in length, made the voyage from New York to Savannah in 57½ hours, according to the *Morning News*, Oct. 14, 1862, ushering in the new era in luxury travel.
13. Ibid., Jan. 8, 9, 15, 1883.

Bibliography

Books and Articles

Appleton's Cyclopaedia of American Biography. New York, 1888+. 7 vols.

Bancroft, Joseph. *Census of the City of Savannah, Together with Statistics Relating to Trade, Commerce, Mechanical Arts, and Health*. . . . Savannah, 1848.

Carter, Clarence E., ed. *Territorial Papers of the United States: Territory of Florida, 1821–1845*. Washington, 1956+. 5 vols.

Chapin, William. *A Complete Reference Gazetteer of the United States of North America* . . . New York, 1843.

Cutler, Henry G. *History of Florida Past and Present, Historical and Biographical*. . . . Chicago, 1923. 3 vols.

Davis, T. Frederick. *History of Jacksonville, Florida and Vicinity, 1513–1924*. St. Augustine, 1925.

Dictionary of American Biography. New York, 1928+. 21+ vols.

Dictionary of American Fighting Ships. Washington, D. C., 1959+. 5 vols.

"Edward C. Anderson: Another Honored Citizen Gone to Rest," Savannah *Morning News*, Jan. 8, 1883.

Ellis, George E. "Recollections of Round Hill School," *Educational Review*, I, 337–44 (Apr., 1891).

Fairbanks, George R. *History of Florida from Its Discovery . . . to the Close of the Florida War*. . . . Philadelphia, 1871.

Giddings, Joshua R. *The Exiles of Florida; or The Crimes Committed by Our Government Against the Maroons Who Fled from South Carolina and Other States*. . . . Columbus, 1858.

Grice, Warren. "The Confederate States Court for Georgia," *Georgia Historical Quarterly*, IX, 131–58 (June, 1925).

———. *The Georgia Bench and Bar*. Macon, 1931.

Hamersly, Thomas H. S., comp. *Complete General Navy Register of the United States from 1776 to 1887*. Washington, 1887.

Harden, William. *A History of Savannah and South Georgia*. Chicago, 1913. 2 vols.

Haskel, Daniel and J. Calvin Smith. *A Complete Descriptive and Statistical Gazetteer of the United States. . . .* New York, 1844.

Heitman, Francis B. *Historical Register and Dictionary of the United States Army from Its Organization. . . . to 1903*. Washington, 1903.

Hoole, W. Stanley. *Four Years in the Confederate Navy: The Career of Captain John Low of the C. S. S. Fingal, Florida, Alabama, Tuscaloosa, and Ajax*. Athens, 1964.

______, ed. *Confederate Foreign Agent: The European Diary of Major Edward C. Anderson*. University, Ala., 1976.

______, ed. "East Florida in 1833: The Letters of Dr. John Durkee," *Florida Historical Quarterly*, LIV, 294–308 (Jan., 1974).

______, ed. "Letters from a Georgia Midshipman on the C. S. S. *Alabama*," *Georgia Historical Quarterly*, LIX, 416–32 (Winter, 1975).

______, ed. "A Visit to the Holy Land in 1837," *Journal of the American Oriental Society*, XCV, 633–44 (Oct.–Dec., 1975).

Howe, M. A. De Wolfe. *Life and Letters of George Bancroft*. New York, 1908. 2 vols.

"Immigration: The French Colony at L' Esperance," Savannah *Morning News*, Apr. 23, 1873.

Johnson, Rossiter, ed. *The Twentieth Century Biographical Dictionary of Notable Americans. . . .* Boston, 1909. 10 vols.

"The Late Edward C. Anderson: Tribute of Respect by the Board of Education," Savannah *Morning News*, Jan. 15, 1883.

Lawrence, Alexander A. *A Present for Mr. Lincoln: The Story of Savannah from Secession to Sherman*. Macon, 1961.

Mahon, John K. *History of the Second Seminole War, 1835–1842*. Gainesville, 1967.

Manucy, Albert C. *The Fort at Frederica.* Tallahassee, 1962.

Martin, Sidney W. *Florida During the Territorial Days.* Athens, 1944.

Moore, Albert B. *History of Alabama.* University, Ala., 1934.

Myers, Robert M., ed. *The Children of Pride: A True Story of Georgia and the Civil War.* New Haven, 1972.

Names of Pupils of Round Hill School, Northampton, Mass., from Its Commencement Until June, 1831. Newport, R. I., 1862.

"Nina Anderson Pape," Savannah *Morning News* and Savannah *Evening Press,* March 6, 1944.

Northampton (Mass.) *Gazette,* 1823–1831.

Outline of the System of Education at the Round Hill School, Present Instructors . . . and . . . Pupils from Its Commencement Until . . . June, 1831. Boston, 1831.

Patrick, Rembert W. *Florida Under Five Flags.* Gainesville, 1945.

Pensacola (Fla.) *Gazette,* 1844–1845.

Porter, Kenneth W. "Billy Bowlegs (Holata Micco) in the Seminole Wars," *Florida Historical Quarterly,* XLV, 219–42 (Jan., 1967).

Powell, W. H. *List of Officers in the United States Army from 1779 to 1900. . . .* New York, 1900.

Prospectus of a School To Be Established at Round Hill, Northampton, Mass. . . . by Joseph G. Cogswell and George Bancroft. Cambridge, 1823.

Read, William A. *Florida Place-Names of Indian Origin and Seminole Personal Names.* Baton Rouge, 1934.

Reynolds, Charles B. *Old St. Augustine: The Story of Three Centuries.* St. Augustine, 1885.

Scharf, J. Thomas. *History of the Confederate States Navy from Its Organization to the Surrender of the Last Vessel.* New York, 1887.

Sinclair, Arthur. *Two Years on the Alabama.* Boston, 1895.

Some Account of the School for Liberal Education of Boys Established at Round Hill, Northampton, Mass., by Joseph G. Cogswell and

George Bancroft. Northampton, 1826.
"The School at Northampton," *United States Literary Gazette*, I, 331–32 (Feb. 15, 1825).
Sprague, John T. *Origin, Progress, and Conclusion of the Florida Wars. . . .* New York, 1848.
Testimony Taken by the Joint Select Committee to Inquire Into the Condition of Affairs in the Late Insurrectionary States: The Ku Klux Klan Conspiracy. Washington, 1872.
Tichnor, Anna Eliot, ed. *Life of Jos. Green Cogswell as Sketched in His Letters*. Boston, 1874.
War of the Rebellion Records: A Compilation of the Official Records of the Union and Confederate Armies. Washington, 1880–1901. 121 vols.
Wells, Tom Henderson. *The Slave Ship Wanderer*. Athens, 1967.
Westcott, Allan. "Commodore Jesse D. Elliott, A Stormy Petrel of the Navy," *United States Naval Institute Proceedings*, LIV, 773–78 (Sept., 1928).
Williams, John Lee. *The Territory of Florida, or Sketches of the Topography, Civil and Natural History . . . from the First Discovery to the Present Time*. New York, 1837.

Manuscripts

The Edward Clifford Anderson Collection, on loan to the University of North Carolina, Chapel Hill, consists of the diaries and fifty-odd letters, and the Schwalb Collection, owned by Anderson's great-granddaughter, Mrs. Florence Crane Schwalb, of Savannah, includes numerous pictures, official documents, letters, and miscellany. Copies of the more significant items are in The University of Alabama Library, Tuscaloosa.

"The Historical Links in the Chain of Title to Lebanon Plantation on Little Ogeechee River in Chatham County, Georgia," a typescript, is in possession of Dr. and Mrs. Howard J. Morrison, of Savannah.

The official records of Edward Clifford Anderson during

his service in the United States Navy (1833–1849) and in the Confederate States Army (1861–1865) are in the National Archives, Washington, D. C.

The numerous letters, papers, photocopies, and other material assembled in the preparation of this monograph are in The University of Alabama Library.

Acknowledgments

PUTTING THIS BOOK TOGETHER, EVEN THOUGH A SMALL ONE, could not have been done without the help of many people, too many to mention here. But I do want especially to thank the following who befriended me far beyond the call of duty:

Mrs. J. Fred (née Florence Crane) Schwalb, not only for permission to use the Anderson papers on loan to the University of North Carolina Library and in her private possession, but also for her generous cooperation;

Mrs. Lilla M. Hawes, director of the Georgia Historical Society Library, for her guidance and assistance in securing and copying needed documents;

Judge Alexander A. Lawrence, author of *A Present for Mr. Lincoln . . .*, for lending me material, checking my manuscript, and escorting me about historical Savannah and Chatham County;

W. Porter Kellam, director emeritus, University of Georgia Library, for his many favors—and, especially, for his friendship over the long years;

Dr. and Mrs. Howard J. Morrison, of Savannah, present owners of Lebanon, for supplying me with pertinent documents, maps, and photographs and for their hospitality in their historic home;

Dr. J. Isaac Copeland, director emeritus of the Southern Collection, University of North Carolina Library, and his altruistic co-workers for their courteous professional help;

The University of Alabama Library Staff, particularly

Mrs. Catherine T. Jones, Mrs. Frances P. Barton, Mrs. Tera M. Biddle, Mrs. Frankie Thomas, Mrs. Joyce H. Lamont, and Derek S. Milsom, for their friendly assistance;

Mrs. Addie S. Hoole, my good wife, who shared with me the frustrations of research and served simultaneously as my typist, proofreader, and severest critic; and last (but obviously first),

President David Mathews, The University of Alabama, and the members of the University Research Grants Committee, whose generosity made this study possible, and especially to their efficient executive secretary, Mary E. Jackson, whose constant and cordial cooperation often converted what might have been unpleasant chores into genuinely cheerful accomplishments.

THE UNIVERSITY OF ALABAMA W. STANLEY HOOLE

Index

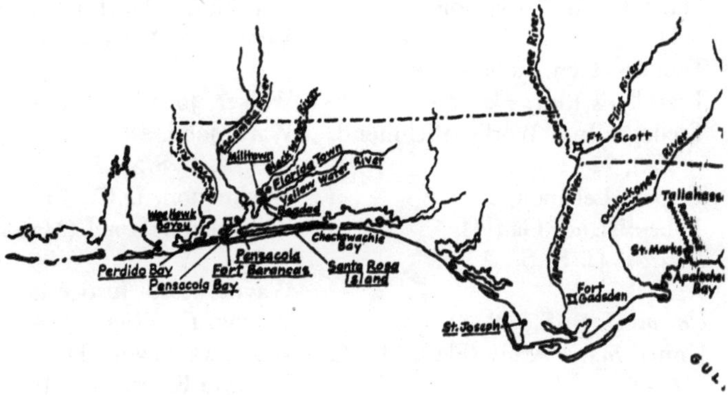

SKETCH
OF
FLORIDA TERRITORY, 1844

PLACES MENTIONED BY
MASTER EDWARD C. ANDERSON
ARE UNDERLINED

0 20 40 60 80 100
MILES

By Glenn W. House, 1976

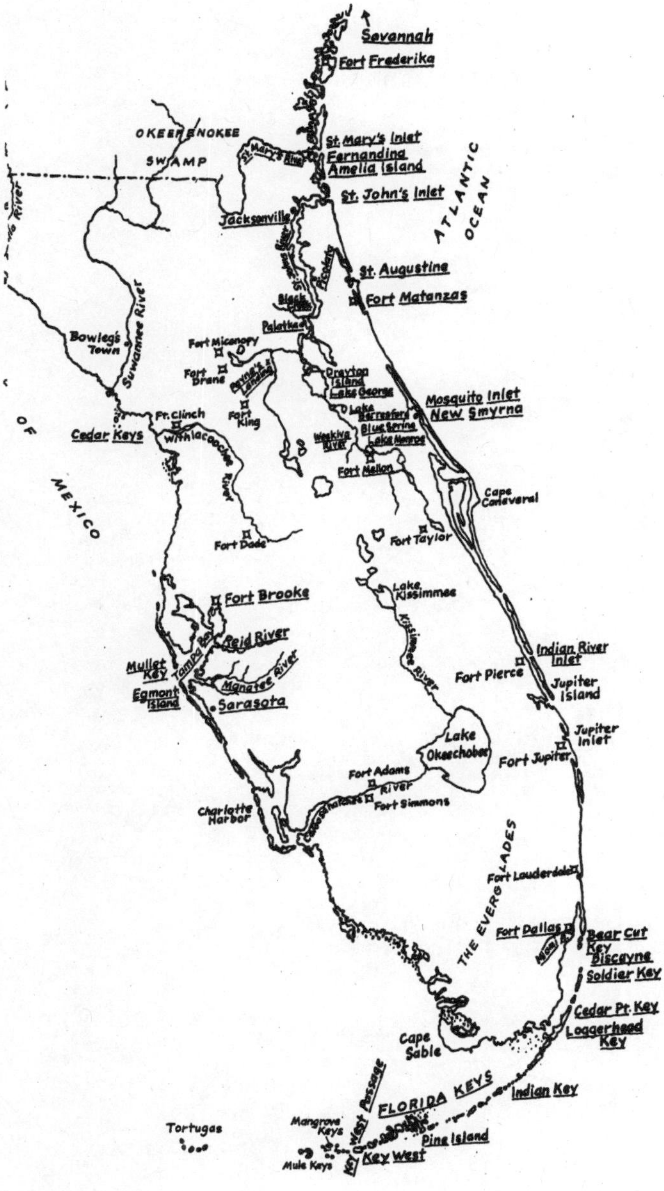

Savannah
Fort Frederika
OKEEFENOKEE
SWAMP
St. Mary's River
St. Mary's Inlet
Fernandina
Amelia Island
St. John's Inlet
ATLANTIC
OCEAN
Jacksonville
St. John's River
Picolata
St. Augustine
Fort Matanzas
Black Creek
Palatka
Bowleg's Town
Suwannee River
Fort Micanopy
Fort Drane
Payne's Landing
Fort King
Drayton Island
Lake George
Lake Beresford
Blue Spring
Lake Monroe
Wekiva River
Fort Mellon
Mosquito Inlet
New Smyrna
Pt. Clinch
Cedar Keys
Withlacoochee River
OF
MEXICO
Cape Canaveral
Fort Dade
Fort Taylor
Lake Kissimmee
Fort Brooke
Reid River
Tampa Bay
Mullet Key
Egmont Island
Manatee River
Sarasota
Kissimmee River
Indian River Inlet
Fort Pierce
Jupiter Island
Jupiter Inlet
Lake Okeechobee
Fort Jupiter
Fort Adams
River
Fort Simmons
Charlotte Harbor
Caloosahatchee
THE EVERGLADES
Fort Lauderdale
Fort Dallas
Miami R.
Bear Cut
Key Biscayne
Soldier Key
Cedar Pt. Key
Loggerhead Key
Cape Sable
FLORIDA KEYS
Indian Key
Key West Passage
Mangrove Keys
Tortugas
Mule Keys
Pine Island
Key West

Drawings by
Edward C. Anderson

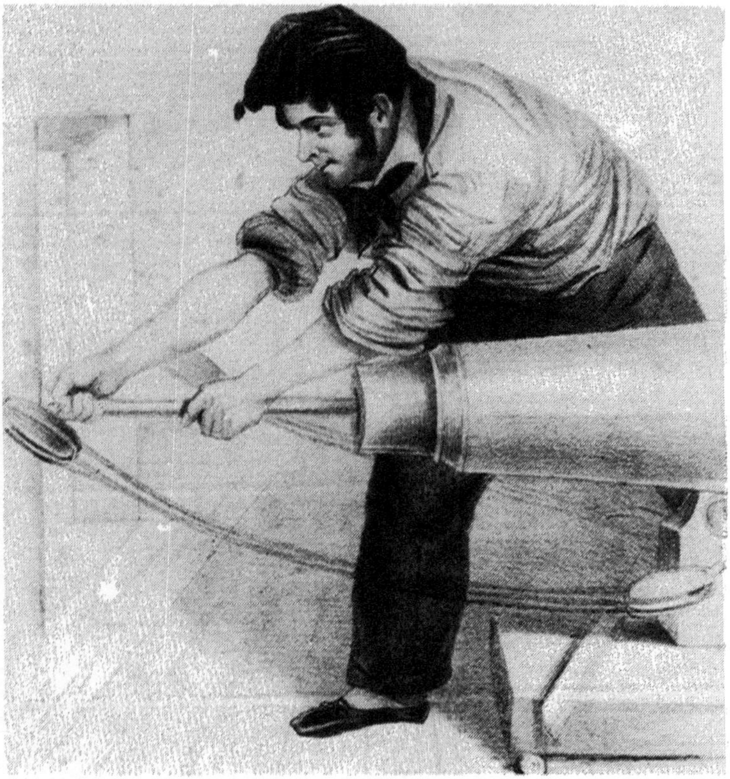

A CANNONEER ABOARD *LEXINGTON*

UNIDENTIFIED LADY (1843)